THE ORIGINAL HOUSE WHERE THE ILLUSTRIOUS LOTT
CAREY WAS BORN IN 1780

It is located about thirty-five miles from the City of Richmond, Va. The lumber for the building was obtained by use of the whipsaw. The well in the foreground is of recent origin; Lott Carey got water from a spring. Sitting in front of the building is the late Rev. Dr. Evans Payne, pastor of the Fourth Baptist Church, Richmond, Va. He has some friends with him. The two ladies standing in the door were owners of the property at the time the photograph was taken. This picture was secured through the great kindness of Rev. J. W. Kemp, who was pastor of a large Baptist Church in that vicinity.—The Author.

LIBERIA AS I KNOW IT

by

C. C. BOONE, B. D., M. D.

Author of "CONGO AS I SAW IT"

NEGRO UNIVERSITIES PRESS
WESTPORT, CONNECTICUT

916.66032
B724L
155798

Originally published in 1929
Richmond, Virginia

Reprinted 1970 by
Negro Universities Press
A DIVISION OF GREENWOOD PRESS, INC.
WESTPORT, CONN.

SBN 8371-3284-3

PRINTED IN UNITED STATES OF AMERICA

MRS. RACHEL BOONE
Who was for Five Years a Faithful Missionary in Liberia

DEDICATORY

To Mrs. Rachel A. Boone, my devoted and faithful wife, who spent five useful years as consecrated Teacher and Missionary in the Republic of Liberia, is this book affectionately dedicated.

C. C. BOONE.

INTRODUCTION

Interest in Africa is on the increase everywhere. In the past, there have been many legends in circulation about this great Continent. These are giving place to authentic information. Whereas the public was once regaled with vivid stories of the harrowing experiences of Missionaries, we are now beginning to get facts of history, ethnology, commerce, climate, natural resources, tribal government, and prehistoric attainments in civilization.

No spot in Africa is of greater interest to American Negroes than Liberia; both because the present Government was established by American Negroes who migrated to that spot under the patronage of the American Colonization Society, and because it is the one spot in Africa to which the American Negro has unrestricted admission. Liberia is thus the point of free contact between the Negro in America and the Negro in Africa, the avenue through which the American Negro can most easily make his contribution to the development of Africa.

In this volume, Dr. Boone gives authentic information about the historic progress of the Black African Republic. For twenty-six years he has labored in the Congo and in Liberia, whither he went as a Medical Missionary shortly after his graduation from Shaw University. As Pastor of the Providence Baptist Church, in Liberia, which was established by the revered Lott Carey, he had opportunity to become thoroughly acquainted with the history and development of the Negro Republic. The account which he gives of it in this volume should be a part of the education of all the Negro youth of today.

R. R. Moton,

Tuskegee Institute, Alabama.   *Principal.*

FOREWORD

It is with great pleasure that I give to the public this terse statement of my acquaintance with the writer, Rev. C. C. Boone, B. D., M. D., whom I have known for more than twenty-five years.

As a student, he was alert, energetic and untiring in the prosecution of his work. His aptitude and fidelity gave him an unusual stand in the class-room as well as with the entire student body.

He graduated in 1900 from the Virginia Union University, Richmond, Va. He left almost immediately for the Belgian Congo, in West-Central Africa, under the auspices of the Lott Carey Baptist Foreign Mission Society and in co-operation with the American Baptist Foreign Mission Society. There he spent many years of efficient service, having mastered the native language and taught the natives with great effect.

Seeing the great need of medical knowledge, he returned to America and took the medical course at Leonard Medical School, Shaw University, Raleigh, N. C., and went out to Liberia prepared to administer to the needs of both body and soul.

After seven years of relentless toil, the flu epidemic having taken away the only dentist in the Republic, he again returned on furlough and took a dental course at Bodee Dental School, New York City, that thoroughly equipped him to be one of the best-prepared Missionaries ever sent out by any Convention to Africa.

He rendered untiring service to our own Lott Carey Missionaries, traveling often at night in "dug outs" to relieve their sufferings, and was a physician for all the Missionaries and people that desired his service.

He served for many months as Secretary of the American Legation during the absence of Secretary Bundy. His broad education fitted him to perform this service with honor and distinction.

He has given twenty-six years of his life for the betterment of body and soul of the African people in Congo and Liberia.

As Medical Missionary and Chairman of the Board of Control of the Lott Carey Mission in Liberia, I, therefore, commend him most graciously to the public as a man of merit and deeds; I also regard this dissertation on Liberia, Africa, as a worthy and interesting piece of literature.

J. HARVEY RANDOLPH,
Cor. Sec'y Lott Carey Baptist F. M. Society.

Washington, D. C.

PREFACE

I take pleasure in presenting this description of the Liberian Republic to all who desire a true story of conditions existing there. For sixteen years, as Physician in their homes and Pastor of the First Church of the Republic, gave me sufficient insight and data, with other material, to produce this book. To substantiate this fact, I am reproducing below an address and some resolutions. May the blessings of God attend the promulgation of the information herein produced.

I regret that I can not show the picture of that great man. There have been several guesses attempted, but all have utterly failed. He was not a mulatto, but had pure African parents. In his day, men of reputation had tin-types made, but people of Carey's station had no photographs, therefore my inability to present his likeness.

C. C. Boone, M. D.

Note: I have spelled "Lott Carey" this way because the American people spell it that way. It is spelled upon his tombstone "Cary."

AN ADDRESS

By Deacon A. B. Stubblefield

Delivered on behalf of Providence Baptist Church, Monrovia, Liberia, on the occasion of a "send off" in honor of Pastor Clinton C. Boone, M. D., Sunday night, July 25, 1926.

Pastor Boone:

Appearing as I do, in obedience to and fulfillment of an appointment, I may say that although I am pleased to per-

form any duty imposed upon me, yet, it is with a sad heart
that I perform this special task, especially when I consider
the associated circumstances. Still, I am forced to say that
the best friends and acquaintances must part at times.

In reviewing the history of the very first Church of Liberia—Providence Baptist—we find for a memorable period
covering at least 103 years it has been pastored by fifteen
leaders, in the following routine: Rev. Lott Carey, Hilary
Teag, John Day, John T. Richardson, Stephen Britton,
Moore T. Worrell, Joseph A. Johnson, Robert B. Richardson, Thomas H. Tyler, John W. Madison, M. Dela Crusoe,
and Clinton C. Boone. And we all are reminded of the fact
that when the sainted Rev. Lott Carey first pastored, there
was not the slightest thought that you would enjoy the distinction and high honor of being our pastor when we reached a milestone of one hundred years. But God's ways are
past finding out; and it is our strong belief that you, in your
infancy, were "lent to the Lord" by your parents, and the
loan was destined for sea and land; and tonight, after having honestly, faithfully and conscientiously fulfilled your
great and grand mission in Monrovia as our Pastor, we are
offering you in return our esteem and appreciation for
services among us. And also to say good-bye and not farewell, as we cherish a strong hope for your return to us,
through the will of God.

You will recall to memory on the 19th of May, 1919, a
similar program was executed by us, but this was done in
the firm hope of your return to us. You may return, and
you may not, all is enveloped in ignorance. But we hope
and wish most anxiously and fervently your return to us.

We have assembled tonight to express our sincerest feeling of perfect satisfaction with you and your service rendered during your eight years as pastor of the Providence Baptist Church. We are exceedingly proud of you,

because you have been with us and among us; you have led
us through dangers seen and unseen; you have stood by us
at times when the way seemed dark and gloomy; our joys
and sorrows have been yours; and you leave behind living
monuments of the work achieved by you.

I may here remark that there have been times when dis-
agreement set in, but it was for the best. Every man does
not look in the same direction at the same time. We dis-
agreed in our opinions to agree. And amidst all, we can
conscientiously say that everything has worked for the good
of us, your members. Notwithstanding the many difficulties
under which you have labored, you have led an exemplary
life among us.

Brother Pastor, we hate to part with you. We have no
complaint to make against you. You have been faithful in
the performance of your sacred duty. We have not found
you to be "double-tongued." You will always have the
warmest wish for your future continued success cherished
in our bosoms. May God bless you and your efforts. And
we have no doubt that you will always remember us. We
are wedded in fondest satisfaction and hope of continued
success. We trust that God will lead and direct you wherever you go, and may your works here among us follow you.
We offer you the following lines of John Faucett as repre-
senting our continued sincerity:

> Blest be the tie that binds
> Our hearts in Christian love;
> The fellowship of kindred minds
> Is like to that above.
>
> Before our Father's throne
> We pour our ardent prayers;
> Our fears, our hopes, our aims are one,
> Our comforts and our cares.

We share our mutual woes,
Our mutual burdens bear;
And often for each other flows
A sympathizing tear.

When we assunder part,
It gives us inward pain;
But we shall still be joined in heart,
And hope to meet again.

RESOLUTIONS

Adopted by the Board of Managers of the Liberia Baptist
Missionary and Educational Convention, held at Rix In-
stitute July 14, 1926, appreciative of Rev. C. C. Boone,
M. D., of said Board:

Whereas, reviewing the meritorious service rendered in
the Missionary field of the Baptist Church in the Republic
of Liberia by Rev. Clinton C. Boone, M. D., a member of
the Board of Managers of the Liberia Baptist Missionary
and Educational Convention; and

Whereas, not only considering his work in the field as
above mentioned, but also accepting and proclaiming him
as a gentleman of desirable character, hailing from the
United States of America, who fosters every laudable undertaking advanced by both Church and State; and

Whereas, his benevolent services rendered as a medical
doctor among the poor and distressed, executing in the full
the intent and purpose of his missionary spirit; and

Whereas, having served faithfully and honestly as a
member of said Board for a number of years in executing
its missionary and educational aim; and

Whereas, the said Rev. Clinton C. Boone, M. D., being
desirous of visiting his home, friends and relatives in the
United States, which visit will cause his membership and
presence to be vacant; therefore, resolved:

That we record our high appreciation of the services rendered the Board by Rev. Clinton C. Boone, M. D., during his membership.

That the blessing and guidance of the Holy Spirit will direct him throughout his trip to America, and, if possible, may he return to us for future service.

That a copy of these resolutions be sent to him, as well as to some of the leading newspapers for publication.

Respectfully submitted,

REV. W. H. BROOKS, *Ch'n,*
REV. JAS. N. GARNETT,
REV. W. L. SHAW,
Committee.

RESOLUTIONS

Adopted by the Providence Baptist Church and Sunday School, Monrovia, Liberia:

Whereas, it has pleased Almighty God, the Great Missionary of the World, to choose, set apart and ordain as His followers Dr. C. C. Boone and Sister R. A. Boone, his beloved and Christian wife; and

Whereas, immediately upon their arrival here they have unceasingly and untiringly given all of their time and talents in the work of the Master; and

Whereas, during their stay amongst us they have labored as pastor, teachers and Christian leaders; and

Whereas, they have rendered inestimable services to Providence Baptist Church and Sunday School of this city in every way possible; therefore, be it resolved:

First, That we record our highest appreciation for their services and give thanks to Almighty God for such workers.

Second, That as they are about to return to their home in America, that we ask God's divine blessing upon them and their children, that long life, joy, peace and happiness be theirs through their earthly lives.

Third, That they be and are hereby empowered to represent us abroad in any way necessity may demand and serve us in any and every way that they may think beneficial to us.

Fourth, That we commend them and their several families and connections to God to take care of and preserve them, and to return them to Liberia to labor with us.

Further, That a copy of these resolutions be furnished Doctor and Sister Boone and each of the leading newspapers in Liberia, including the Lott Carey Herald, the national voice in America, for publication.

Respectfully submitted,

A. B. STUBBLEFIELD.

THOMAS NORFLEET.

A. B. JOHNSON.

GEO. W. STUBBLEFIELD.

Liberia As I Know It

CHAPTER I

CAUSES THAT LED TO THE FORMATION OF THE REPUBLIC OF LIBERIA

Slavery was not a new institution in 1816. It is an age-old system. It was rocked and nurtured in the cradle of civilization upon the banks of the Nile River; for the nation that reared the giant sphinx that has stood lion-like overlooking the kingdom of Egypt for 5,000 years, that constructed those massive pyramids—that same Hamitic nation of brown and yellow men was the first to hold other men in subjection.

Joseph was the first slave and a forerunner for the salvation of his brethren. If Noah's curse of Caanan or the Hamites was ever fulfilled, certainly they had a long and a glorious period of probation, during which time they carried the arts and sciences to such a high degree of perfection that no other succeeding nation has been able to attain unto it.

The writings of Pliny, Herodotus and Josephus attest the fact that every nation has had its period of subjection to other nations. The "towy-haired Briton was sold upon the auction block of the Romans," says the historian. Hannibal, Caesar and Alexander the Great led thousands of Celts, Gauls, Teutons, Syrians and barbarians behind their victorious chariots of war.

The Pilgrims that formed the first settlement in America held other white men in slavery or serfdom until they had worked and paid their passage. It is stranger than fiction, yet it is true that the very same people who fled from British oppression to America to be free, as soon as they inhaled the first breath of freedom they turned boldly around and enslaved others. The story of ''Evangeline'' sinks into insignificance when compared with ''Uncle Tom's Cabin.''

The slavery of the Negro glared out red upon the horizon because he was the last enslaved, and further because there were so many nations engaged in the nefarious traffic at the same time—England, France, Portugal, Spain and the United States.

I shudder as I stand and gaze at those eighty men chained together, hounded by the slave driver in the Congo, pressed onward by the lacerations of the deadly ''chicot'' into perpetual slavery! Tears unbidden start as I stand at King Gray's town in Liberia and look upon those large rusty cannon used to intimidate the poor captives, and as I turn and peep into that deep cave into which our ancestors were crammed to survive or perish, until the slave ship came by and tore them away from their nursing infants and grayhaired parents! I was compelled to ask, ''Where was God at that time?'' And I think that James Russell Lowell has answered that question:

> Careless seems the Great Avenger:
> History's pages but record
> One death grapple in the darkness,
> 'Twixt old systems and the Word.
> Truth forever on the scaffold,
> Wrong forever on the throne;
> Yet, that scaffold sways the future,
> And behind the dim unknown
> Standeth God within the shadows,
> Keeping watch above His own.

God watched those dejected slaves and guarded their destinies until at last the star of hope shone out above the carnage and night, the silver lining in the cloud appeared. The hearts of men began to soften. They said, ''This thing is not right." Their conscience was mortified at the sight of human beings being dragged away and sold from their children and kindred. "Something must be done," they said. When the New World was waking up to the consciousness of the evil, came the American Revolution, and Virginia, although freighted down with human slavery, made the legislative halls ring with the battle cry, "Give me liberty or give me death"!

Nevertheless, I would not have you ignorant of the fact that thousands of good people in Virginia and many other Southern and Northern States as well, were seeking every way possible to get rid of the blighting curse. Many sweet ladies could never see their slave boys go to sleep at night without teaching them to pray to that God who some day would break their adamantine chains. One boy who was taken back to Africa said, when he knelt down to pray, "Old Misses always had me pray to God before I went to bed."

Could nothing be done? "There had been an uprising in Richmond, Va.," says the Record, "led by two Baptist preachers." And the Virginians, fearing the worst, had appealed to their Governor (Monroe) to send a petition to the President of the United States to find a place where free blacks could be removed from the slaves and colonized by themselves. They suggested Louisiana, behind the Rocky Mountains, and even up in New England; but President Jefferson could not give his sanction to either place mentioned.

Conception of African Colonization

A few Africans who had won their freedom by fighting for England during the Revolutionary War, had found a home in London. But there they could find nothing to do; therefore, they became public beggars. This annoyed the people of London, and Sir Granville Sharpe and Rev. Wil-

liam Wilberforce conceived the idea of returning them to
their home in Africa.

Sierra Leone Established

Agents were sent out to the coast of Africa and a parcel
of ground was purchased from the natives for the colony.
A large party of white and colored persons were sent to begin the settlement.

There were other Negroes that had escaped from the
United States into Canada. These, hearing of the success
of the Sierra Leone party, wished to join them. Accordingly, they were transferred to that place, and among them
was one man, Kizell, of whom you shall hear again.

Paul Cuffey

Paul Cuffey was the son of a white man, but his mother
was an African. Through thrift and industry, he rose to
wealth and influence. He owned a sailing vessel, and with
it visited foreign countries. When he heard of the success
of the Sierra Leone Colony, he desired to pay them a visit.
He offered passage to as many Negroes as desired to accom-
pany him. Forty persons availed themselves of this opportunity, but only eight could pay their own passage. Cuffey
had to defray the expenses of all the others, amounting to
$4,000.

Colonization of American Free Negroes

Two questions agitated the minds of the American people
at this time. One was how to get rid of the free blacks, because they were considered dangerous associates of the
slaved blacks; and the second question that was of much
interest to them was how far a Christian settlement upon
the West Coast of Africa would go towards putting a stop
to the slave trade?

The United States Congress had already passed laws making it a felony to deal in slaves. It had gone so far as to

consider all slaving ships as pirates, to be captured and confiscated. It had sent men-o'-war upon the high seas, around and near the coasts of Africa, to watch and capture all slave vessels whenever possible. But it was stated upon good authority that this measure only irritated the slave traders and accelerated the slave trade. The slavers were of faster speed than the men-o'-war; therefore, when the slavers were chased, many times, they would speed away out of danger, even in the very sight of the men-o'-war. However, the greatest misfortune was that the gunboats could not go on shore to the baracoons where the slaves were imprisoned! Here, hundreds of poor captives fainted, writhed, despaired, died.

There is a story told of one Mr. Samuel Hopkins, who redeemed some slaves and attempted to educate them, with the idea of sending them back to their country. This plan was interrupted by the outbreak of the Revolutionary War. There was, however, one man by the name of Gardner who contrived in some way to get back to Africa, even after he was eighty years old.

Yet, all authors acknowledge that the foremost man in America to advocate the colonization plan was Mr. Robert Finley, of New Jersey. On the 20th of December, 1816, a meeting was held at the home of Mr. Caldwell, in Boston. In this gathering was Mr. Robert Finley, who said, "We must plant a colony of free blacks upon their home soil, Africa, where they can be true men, unoppressed by the prejudice and legislation of the whites." They answered, "Very well, very good. There is only one objection—it can't be done!" Said he, "Very well, we must try."

Another meeting was held in Washington, D. C., and a society was organized, with Mr. Bushrod Washington as the president. He was nephew of President George Washington. In that meeting, it was fully decided to attempt to colonize the free Negroes of the United States upon the West Coast of Africa.

The country must be surveyed and a suitable section obtained for this purpose. Who would undertake this arduous task? One man by the name of Mills offered himself, and he secured as his companion Mr. Ebenezer Burgess. They received their commissions and sailed on the 16th of November, 1816. They had instructions to proceed by the way of England. Near the English coast, they encountered a terrific storm. The masts of the ship were cut away, and the captain and his two sons were lost as they sought to desert the ship. Mills and Burgess prayed unceasingly to Almighty God for succor in that perilous hour. God heard their prayer and rescued the ship from destruction and it drifted upon the coast of France. Without any further difficulty, the Missionaries reached London.

They were greeted joyously in London by Messrs. Sharpe and Wiberforce, who gave them valuable information and assistance for their mission. Mills and Burgess soon said good-bye to their friends in London and set out again to complete their journey. After a very pleasant trip down the coast, they soon disembarked at Sierra Leone.

They were delighted with the beauty of the tropics, and at once began to negotiate for the territory from the natives. They were greatly assisted in this by the man Kizell, who had come from Canada. He took them to his home, Sherbo or Campellar, and introduced them to his King. They succeeded in securing an excellent plot of land for the undertaking. Their business finished, they quickly re-embarked for America.

On the return journey, Mr. Mills died and was buried at sea. Mr. Burgess was received in America with great enthusiasm.

CHAPTER II

FOUNDING OF THE COLONY

In 1819, Congress passed an act giving the President of the United States authority to seize any Africans that were being smuggled into the country contrary to law and to take them back to their homes in Africa. A freight vessel, the Elizabeth, was chartered for that purpose, which was to be accompanied by the war sloop Cyane. This expedition was fitted up at the expense of the American government. They had no mind of establishing a colony at this time. They were simply instructed to build a receptacle at the place where Mills and Burgess had selected the territory and to place here any recaptured Africans until their home and people could be located and they could be returned to them.

In this instance, the Colonization Society grasped the opportunity to send out some extra families to begin the settlement that they had so long contemplated. They had often appealed to Congress for help and co-operation in this matter without success; now this was their chance. Thirty families, making eighty-eight persons, gladly sought to go.

Farewell in New York

They met in New York at the African Baptist Church at an early hour for a farewell meeting, but there was so much confusion the services had to be abandoned and the emigrants secretly conveyed to the steamer. After being placed on board the ship, then, there was so much excitement that they were compelled to remove the ship from the wharf out into the harbor. Here it became ice-bound for two weeks. It finally sailed in February, 1820.

The prophetic words of the poet come in place here:

> O Thou, who built Jerusalem
> For Israel's wandering race,
> And yet in love will gather them
> Back to their dwelling-place;
>
> Who captive Joseph, like a flock
> Led forth with prowess high,
> And gave them water from the rock
> And manna from the sky—
>
> Smile on our efforts who shall fain
> Redeem each outcast slave,
> And waft them to that land again,
> Thou to their father's grave.
>
> They seek a better country,
> Their toils and cares shall cease;
> Build Thou their city, grant them there
> A heritage of peace.
>
> Thy name, O Christ, and Thine alone
> Is all their hope and trust;
> Be Thou their precious Corner-stone,
> To raise their walls from dust.
>
> Thy Spirit's sword unto them lent,
> Thy cross their banner free;
> Thy word their only battlement,
> And faith their victory.
>
> Their watchmen shall lift up their voice,
> Together shall they sing,
> And in the guardian care rejoice
> Of Israel's sleepless King.
>
> The little one, men's scoff and scorn,
> A mighty realm shall be,
> And generations yet unborn
> Shall give the praise to Thee.

—Rev. George W. Bethune.

Landing at Sierra Leone.

Without any event of importance after forty days, the voyage ended, and they cast anchor at Sierra Leone, West Africa. The sight of the "Fatherland" was very thrilling to some, while others expressed disapproval of the slave ships and many other unsightly spectacles which met their every gaze. They were cordially received by the Colonists of Sierra Leone and rendered all the assistance possible. The man Kizell, for whom they looked here and there, was hard to find. However, after much searching they found him.

Why the Colony Failed at Sherbo

He took them to his home, Campellar or Shebro, and made them as comfortable as he could. Instead of taking them to his King Sherbo and saying to him, "These be them men who get that land for the 'Merican people, they come now"; he took them to see the son of the King, Couber. Messrs. Bacon and Bankson, for the Government, and Dr. Samuel Crozier, for the Colonization Society, had not been in the habit of asking the permission of a Negro for anything; therefore, they patted Kizell on the back and began landing their cargo without proper permission from the King. Certainly, when they approached him then about the purchased property, he knew nothing of it. All of us know, when entering a district in Africa, if you fail to get permission from the Paramount Chief, all of your labors in that vicinity are in vain. When I read of all the agents dying except Bacon, I was not surprised. I have no doubt the African people, insulted because the agents had not respected their King, showed them a bad spring of water intentionally. There is also intimation of the fact that there were secret influences at work with the natives against the settlement at Sherbo, because it was too close to the Sierra Leone Colony.

Sickness and Death

In a very few days, thirty or forty of the emigrants were sick with fever. The ships could not be taken up to Sherbo, and a small sailing vessel was purchased to take as many as could be carried and their cargo. This resulted in much hardship and fatigue to the emigrants. Those that went ahead to Sherbo were nearly all sick and dying. Dr. Crozier, the Physician, was upon the boat behind, and could not be reached. In this sad predicament, they made every effort to reach Dr. Crozier. And when they did find him, he, too, was prostrated with fever. Bankson and Winn, Government Agents, died. Dr. Crozier died. Mr. Bacon, to escape a similar fate, returned to the United States. Rev. Daniel Koker, a colored man, of the Episcopal Church, was left in charge of the Colony.

Many were the trials of those early days, and he had upon his hands some sick, many stealing, many complaining, many dying. Notwithstanding all of those vexing besetments, Rev. Daniel Koker sent home this burning message: "Let the colored people come up to the help of the Lord; let nothing discourage the colored people." So perplexing were the problems that daily confronted him, that he had often to resort to the Governor of Sierra Leone for advice and assistance.

Conference

Upon the ship Nautilus, there came out also as agent for the Government Rev. Mr. Bacon (nephew of the first Bacon), and Mr. Wiltberger came as agent of the Colonization Society. By a conference with the agents and Mr. Koker, it was decided to remove from Sherbo. They consulted the Governor of Freetown Sierra Leone, and he granted them permission to occupy a place not far distant from their own Colony called Foura Bay, until they could secure land.

CHAPTER III

Foura Bay—Grand Bassa—Mesurado

Foura Bay.

Prominent among the new arrivals since the departure of Mr. Bacon was Dr. Eli Ayers, who came out upon the Shark, in July, 1821; in fact, he was at Sherbo with Rev. Koker and was of great assistance with the sick and discouraged. Sherbo was an island, and it was so low that when the waters of the ocean were at floodtide, the island was almost entirely inundated. Therefore, the remaining Colonists were speedily removed to Foura Bay, where the elevation was higher and the surroundings more salubrial.

Seeking a New Home

Having repaired the sailing vessel which Mr. Bacon had purchased to carry the Colonists to Sherbo, he and Mr. Andrus decided to go in search of a new home. Accordingly, they sailed out from Sierra Leone in a southeasternly direction and landed at a place known as Grand Cape Mount. They were not so favorably impressed with this section of the country, so continued their journey southward. About sixty miles from Cape Mount, they spied a high bluff. They landed and sought to hold a "palaver" with the King, but he would have nothing to do with them.

Grand Bassa

Continuing their voyage, some two days afterward, they reached Bassa Cove, now known as Grand Bassa. Here they were cordially received by the King and hospitably entertained by the people. They talked the matter over with the King and bargained for a section of his country. During their sojourn in that portion of the country, they were helped and courteously conducted about the town by one Cru man named "Bottle Beer."

Mesurado Secured by Stockton and Ayers

Captain Stockton came out for the Government upon the sloop Alligator. Now, there were so many at Foura Bay that Dr. Ayers and the Captain agreed to try their wits at securing a site for the Colony. Sailing southeast down the coast, they came in sight of the high bluff known as Cape Mesurado. Dr. Ayers said, "That is the place we ought to have." Captain Stockton replied, "We must have it."

At the King's Palace

Captain Stockton and Dr. Ayers went ashore and sought an audience with the King, but they were informed that the King at the Cape had no authority to hold a big palaver with them, and that they would have to go into the country to the Palace of the Big King. Although the natives were treacherous and the trails were filled with saw-grass and hanging vines, they decided to go. When they arrived at the Palace of the King, about eight miles distant from Mesurado, and had seated themselves, they heard many expressions that tended to stir up strife among the people. "Them be the same people fussing at Sherbo." Another man yelled out, "Dese theme people who break up our slave trade." When the King came in, he scowled at them and quickly demanded of them their business in his dominion. Things began to look critical. Captain Stockton moved his seat beside the King, and when they really tried to assault them, Stockton exhibited his firearms, and all was quietude at once. They then held a palaver with the King and his Chiefs and purchased the Cape.

The following Kings signed for the country: King Peter X (his mark), King George X (his mark), King Long Peter X (his mark), King Governor X (his mark), King Jimmy X (his mark). Captain Stockton signed for the Government, and Dr. Ayers for the Colonization Society.

Settling at Mesurado

As soon as the negotiations were finished and a part of the purchase price had been paid, they hastened away to impart the good news and remove the Colonists.

Purchase of "Perseverance Island"

Before leaving the Cape, they purchased a small island adjacent to the Cape. This island was owned by one John Mills, a half-breed, who had been to England and was now back, evidently engaged in the slave trade.

Danger and Treachery

The emigrants were brought, consisting mostly of young men, while the women and children were left until another time. They were forced to land upon Perseverance Island because, while they were gone to Foura Bay, the natives had changed their minds and wanted to withdraw their terms for the sale of the Cape. Furthermore, there were no houses available upon the Cape, but there were a few thatched huts upon the Island.

They could not secure wood and water upon the Island, and were compelled to take a canoe and go down Stockton Creek (so named for Captain Stockton) and get these things. To this the natives also objected, and often hid in ambush along the banks and attacked them. Once they seriously injured one of the Colonists.

There was so much complaint and dissatisfaction that Dr. Ayers sought to confer again with the King upon the matters of the Colony. When he had reached the Palace of the King, he was immediately taken prisoner and held until he agreed to leave the Cape.

King Boatswain

Living far away in the interior was one Boatswain. He had been to England and fought in the English Army. He

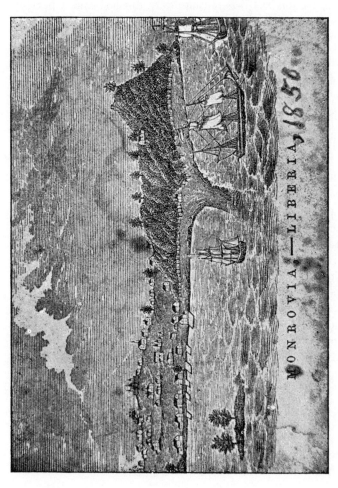

Monrovia, Liberia, in 1850

was friendly towards the " 'Mericans.'' He swayed a controlling influence over the country. His assistance was sought by the Colonists, and when the matter had been fully explained to him he took sides with the emigrants. He ordered the Kings to accept the remainder of their pay for the land. And upon departing cautioned the native Kings not to let him hear any more of them, adding, ''If you do, I will settle it with your heads.''

The Dey people were highly incensed at King Peter for selling their land, and threatened to hang him. Had it not been for the timely intervention of King Boatswain, he might have lost his head.

Mesurado Occupied

The Colonists, after many hindrances, however, removed to Cape Mesurado on April 25, 1822, and immediately raised the American Flag.

Rains and Hardships

The rains were falling in torrents, and they were almost without food. Many were sick, and others were discouraged. All the Agents had died, leaving only Dr. Ayers; and he, seeing the Colony in such a hopeless condition, lost faith in the undertaking and returned to Sierra Leone. A few of the emigrants accompanied him, but Lott Carey was firmly set in his conviction to remain. He said, ''Here I have come, and here I shall remain.'' (This saying has been attributed to Elijah Johnson, but in the African Repository Lott Carey is spoken of as having said these words. Doubtless, Elijah Johnson and Lott Carey were both determined to remain.) It is supposed that Daniel James had charge of affairs at this time. Rev. Daniel Koker is lost in the narrative; some say he remained at Sierra Leone.

CHAPTER IV

ASHMUN AND THE COLONISTS

Mr. Jehudi Ashmun, Agent of the Colonization Society, reached Mesurado in August, 1822. A man in Georgia had manumitted all of his forty-five slaves, and Mr. Ashmun had been appointed to take them back to their home. He was surprised to find all of the Agents gone, but very favorably impressed with the appearance of the settlement.

Colony Under Colored People

The colored men, with a few cumbersome tools, had erected thirty dwelling-houses and built a large storehouse. They had also felled the trees and made a large clearing for the village.

Shipwreck and Fire

About this time, an English gunboat had brought into harbor a slaver with many slaves upon it. In attempting to run in to land them, the boat ran aground. The natives, who claim all wrecks as their own, rushed down to seize their prize, and the Captain fired upon them. Finally, seeing their determination, asked assistance from the Colony. This was speedily rendered, and the brass fieldpiece was opened upon them, which sent them away panic-stricken. Mr. Ashmun also had trouble. His ship parted her cable and was almost driven to destruction upon the beach. It was at last anchored and was then found to be at least five miles from land. Mr. Ashmun and his wife came ashore, but the cargo had to remain upon the ship for many months, as firing the cannon had practically destroyed the storehouse with the most of the goods it contained. As soon as Mr. Ashmun reached the Colony, and upon hearing the many complaints of the natives, he began at once to make preparations of defense.

Regulations for Defense.

Mr. Ashmun began at once the erection of the Martel Tower, to be used as a watch tower and for the protection of the military stores. The following military organization was effected by Elijah Johnson, who had fought in the American Revolutionary War:

1. The settlement is under military law.

2. Elijah Johnson Commissary of Stores.

3. R. Sampson is Commissary of Ordnance.

4. Lott Carey, Health Officer, Government Inspector.

5. F. James is Captain of Brass Mounted Fieldpiece, and has assigned to his command R. Newport, M. S. Draper, William Mead, and J. Adams.

6. A. James is Captain of the Long Eighteen and has under him J. Benson, E. Smith, William Hollongs, D. Hawkins, John and Thomas Spencer.

7. John Shaw is Captain of the Southern Picket Station, mountaing two iron guns. To his command are attached S. Campbell, E. Jackson, J. Lawrence, L. Crook and George Washington.

8. D. George is Captain of the Eastern Picket Station, mounting two iron pieces. Aattached to him are E. Edmondson, Joseph Gardiner, Josiah Webster and Jonas Carey (relative of Lott).

9. C. Brander is Captain of Carriage, mounting two swivels to act in concert with brass piece, and to move from station to station as occasion may require. Attached to him are T. Tines and L. Buttler.

10. Every man to have his musket and ammunition with him, even when at the large guns.

11. Every officer is responsible for the conduct of the men placed under him, who are to obey him at their peril.

12. The guns are to be gotten ready for action immediately and every effective man to be employed at the pickets.

13. Five stations to be occupied with guard at night until orders shall be given.

14. No useless firing permitted.

15. In case of alarm, every man is to repair at once to his post and do his duty.

Condition of Mr. Ashmun

Mr. Ashmun himself was in a perilous condition, and having been bereaved of his dear companion in September, he was left alone to fight the fever and the natives. He tried to do his best, but most of the time he was confined to his bed and was compelled to send out his orders from his bed chamber.

Tense Condition in the Colony

This was the time when heart and patience were fully tried. The rains were pouring down, and not sufficient shelter for the sick women and children. Poorly equipped, with only thirty-five men capable of bearing arms, thirteen of whom had never loaded a gun, with very little ammunition, very little food, surrounded by dense forest that could be used as hiding places for the enemy, they trusted and waited.

War! War!

There was every indication of an impending conflict. In fact, one Bassa man named Ba Kai came secretly at night and whispered to the guards and told them to stand by their guns; said he, "War in four days." The natives had mobilized upon Bushrod Island, opposite the Cape. In a

few days they could be seen stealing over on the Cape side
at night and concentrating about a half-mile from the
Colony.

The Guards Off Duty

The guards were advised never to leave their posts until
sunrise. The natives were watching from the thick bush,
and when, on the 11th of December, 1822, they discovered
that the guards had left their posts before the others replaced them, the natives fired, gave the war yell and rushed
into the breach. Several men were wounded, one mortally,
and if the natives had pushed their conquest instead of pil-
laging for loot, they might have gained an easy victory.
The soldiers, excited and surprised, forsook their guns; but
Lott Carey, the hero of the occasion, rallied their broken
forces and the enemy was driven back.

Entreaties in Vain

Captain Brassey, of Liverpool, passing at the time, shared
his stores with the Colonists and did what he could to dis-
arm the warring tribesmen, but in vain. They had determined to attack the Colonists on the 30th of November, but
they delayed until Captain Brassey was gone. With nothing more to fear, early on the 1st day of December, 1822,
with the little palisade entirely surrounded, they rushed
onward and attacked from all sides. The soldiers were on
guard and fought bravely this time, but it was plainly seen
that they would not be able to hold out very long against
such an innumerable host.

Matilda New Port

When the battle was fast going in favor of the natives,
when only fourteen men remained at their posts, when already many women and children had been taken prisoners,
Matilda Newport, one of that number, seeing conditions of

things, asked permission to smoke her pipe. The request
granted, she stealthily fumbling about the big brass field-
piece that had been captured, dropped a coal upon the fuse,
which shot a hole through the line of the enemy and sent
them terrified into retreat.

Not many historians have given Matilda Newport credit
for this great victory. Mr. Ashmun, in describing the battle, says, ''At this time, a big gun was uncovered on the
east side.'' Miss Irene Gant, A. B., speaking for the women
of Liberia on the First day of December, 1916, said, in part:
''Matilda Newport is Liberia's Joan of Arc. Ninety years
ago, when our thirty-five settlers, sixteen of whom were
emaciated, and therefore useless, would have been completely exterminated when Safety had apparently shrunk from
her duty to those who needed her most, when defeat to our
forces would have meant annihilation of our band, death to
the embryonic State—then it was that our noble Matilda,
seeing the handful of men dispirited, observing the shatter-
ed condition of affairs, and the gloom of despondency which
the menacing advance of the natives had cast upon the lives
of the pioneers, stepped forth and lighted that cannon before the lines of the enemy, which spelled, in the glorious
reverberation of its blast, ''Possibility.'' We are sorry that
she got this fire from her ''pipe,'' but the deed was heroic
and her name shall live as long as Liberia lives. Other
women have done excellently, but thou, Matilda, excellest
them all! Hon. Edwin Barclay, Secretary of State, sings
to her in the following lines:

> O truest type of womankind!
> The echoing blast that from the deep
> And pregnant cannon's roar now find
> Their solemn way down the deep declivity of time,
> Shall nerve thy sons, thy daughters thrill,
> In hours of darkness and of ill.

Monument Erected to the Memory of Matilda
Newport, who Saved Liberia with her Pipe

Thou, woman, art sublime!
Heroic in thy deeds, supreme through time,
Rising above all mortal fears,
Scorning the threats of foe,
The tears perchance of friends;
Viewing in dreams the bright innumerable beams.

Light that, flashing from your hand devoted,
Should o'er flood the strand
Where Niger runs his stately course:
Thou didst thy duty, and by force of determined aim,
Thou laidest deep the foundation of the State
Which to thee unknown thou madest.

Live long, the mother of thy country's conquerors!
Live bright ensample when the darkness lowers!
And in the nearing future, when this land
Shall rise to powers supreme and to command,
Thy glorious virtues shall her daughters share,
Her sons make valor their sincerest care!

The colonists were in a fearful state of affairs after the
battle. Many were wounded; one woman, Anna Hawkins,
receiving thirteen wounds; Mr. Ashmun had three bullets
to pass through his coat, but without effect. But not all his
fellow-soldiers met with such fortunate results. Lott Carey,
the self-taught physician, was in need of surgical instruments to properly treat the wounds of the complaining soldiers. Their food also had practically exhausted, and they
had now been placed upon a very strict ration; besides,
they had only about three rounds of ammunition. The natives were constantly lurking around, planning another
attack. The guards kept their posts each night. Mr. Ashmun, writing to the Society, said, "Send us help speedily,
or be prepared for the greatest earthly calamity."

Midshipman Gordon

Just at that time, Major Laing was steaming down the
coast near Liberia, when one of the guards, frightened at

some peculiar noise, fired a cannon. Major Laing anchored
his ship in the harbor and sent a messenger on shore to
ascertain the cause of the firing. To their surprise, they
found the struggling Colonists in the peril of their lives.
They did not know that a settlement of civilized people had
been made there.

When they reported the matter to Major Laing, he sent
Midshipman Gordon and twelve seamen to remain and assist the Colonists until another ship should pass and take
the sailors to their homes. They brought food, and ammunition for the guns. The sailors made themselves busy
by helping the emigrants build their houses.

This put an end to the war. The native Kings sent back
the children that had been taken prisoners of their own ac-
cord. Sorry to relate, however, that Midshipman Gordon
and his twelve seamen fell victims to the malarial fever,
and their bodies were interred in the soil at Monrovia.

Fever and Dissatisfaction

Dr. Ayers came back and relieved Mr. Ashmun of the
Colonial duties, but this did not last long, because the fever
was again sapping away his life and he was compelled to
return immediately to the United States. Mr. Ashmun was
once more called into service. When the war was over and
the Colonists resumed their labors upon their homes and
farms, a spirit of rebellion arose among the settlers. Ashmun says that Lott Carey was the leader. They were clam-
oring for a voice in the affairs of the Colony. Said they,
''We have come here to be free, and nothing short of real
freedom will suffice.'' They claimed that Mr. Ashmun with-
held their food and took the best of everything for himself.
He must have a fine house in which to live, while they were
compelled to abide in thatch-houses, and they desired a voice
in the conduct of the village. Mr. Ashmun's failing health

caused him to take a vacation at Cape Verde Islands, but the Colonists registered their complaints with the Board in America. Some naval officers, passing the Cape about that time, went to America and confirmed what the colonists had said.

The Board, feeling that these matters should be adjusted, sent Mr. Gurley to make a survey of the case. Passing Cape Verde and finding Mr. Ashmun, he persuaded him to return and reviewed the situation with him. When Mr. Gurley arrived and held a palaver with Lott Carey and the other leaders of the Colony, he found much cause for their complaints.

A code of laws was established and the citizens were asked to elect a Council to associate with the Agent in the government of the Colony. When the election was held, Lott Carey was chosen Vice-Agent. Peace and satisfaction re-established, the people began to build their houses and cultivate their farms. Mr. Ashmun, seeing the prosperity of the settlement and feeling that he must go to America to save his life, departed, leaving Lott Carey, Vice-Agent, in charge of affairs. When he went to Cape Verde, he left Ilijiah Johnson in charge.

CHAPTER V

Lott Carey was born in 1780, at Charles City, Va., some thirty miles from the City of Richmond. His father was an ardent Christian and a consistent member of the Baptist Church in Richmond, Va. His mother was a quiet, godly woman, but doubtless never had an opportunity to join any Church. His father belonged to one man by the name of Christian. Lott was their only child. And it may be inferred from the above information that Lott was brought up under wholesome influences.

Working in Richmond, Va.

In the year 1804, when he was just twenty-four years of age, he was brought to Richmond and hired out to work in the tobacco factory as a common laborer in the Shockoe Tobacco Warehouse. At that time, he was as "wild as a sinner could be." Instead of getting better, he grew continually worse; but, like Saul of Tarsus, he was a chosen vessel of the Lord and destined to take a prominent part in one of the noblest enterprises of his day. Having been convinced of his "lost and ruined condition," he turned to the Lord, and, with full purpose of heart, was baptized by Rev. John Courteny and was received that year (1807) as a member of the First Baptist Church, Richmond, Va.

Lott Carey, while endowed with intellectual capabilities, had not attended school. Schools were unknown for his people in those dark days. Once, while he was listening to the reading of the 3rd chapter of John, he was seized with a desire to know to read. In some unknown way, he obtained a book and continued to struggle, being often instructed by the young white men who were working in the factory with him, until he was at last able to read for himself. In the same way, by dint of courage, he learned to write. Immediately after obtaining a knowledge of books, he began to hold meetings and warn sinners to "flee from the wrath to come."

The Church, observing that he had gifts to be useful, encouraged him to use them in preaching the Gospel. He spent all his extra moments in reading every book that he could obtain. He not only read the Bible, which was his principal textbook, but he read political economy. One day he was also found reading Smith's "Wealth of Nations."

He was now constantly engaged in preaching the Gospel in Richmond and all the surrounding country. Collin Teag, who was also entering the ministry, traveled with Carey and made tours from Lynchburg, Va., to Norfolk and the surrounding country. Once while preaching in Norfolk, he referred to Liberia as a "free country." (Young J. J. Roberts heard it, and that was just what he had longed to know. Roberts emigrated there and became the first President of the Republic.)

His services at the tobacco warehouse were highly appreciated. He was put in charge of the shipments, or was what we call now the shipping clerk. It has been said of him that, although trusted with many casks of tobacco, so efficiently did he do his work that he could account for any cask immediately. This so elated his employers that they often compensated him with an extra five-dollar bill. They also allowed him to sell, for his own benefit, any waste tobacco that might drop around the warehouse in the rudiments of shipping. By carefully saving these little crumbs that fell into his hands, he was able to ransom his two sons and himself for $850. His dear companion had died some time before, and he married a second wife the daughter of R. Sampson, of Petersburg.

Emigration

As soon as the journal of the tour of Mills and Burgess had been published, the mind of Lott Carey and that of his co-worker were made up to go to Africa. He was now receiving a regular salary, which was increased from time to time until it amounted to $800 per year. While in Richmond he stirred up such an interest in Africa that a Foreign Mission Society was established in the Baptist Church. This Society raised from year to year over $100 for the redemption of Africa.

When the owners of the factory heard that Lott Carey contemplated going to Africa, they at once raised his wages; but he could not be bought with money. The desire to go in person and carry the blessed Gospel to the benighted heathen was like fire in his bones. A great struggle existed between this desire and his personal interest. He was now in possession of a snug little farm near Richmond, was receiving a handsome salary, and his reputation as high as he could wish. Besides, he was the object of universal affection among his own people as a preacher. There were also some discouraging circumstances in relation to Africa. The facilities for laboring there were few and the climate was sickly, but none of these things could deter him from engaging in his God-given calling.

When asked by a brother-minister how he could think of quitting a position of so much ease and comfort and encounter the dangers of an African wilderness, he replied, "I am an African, and in this country, however meritorious my conduct, and resectable my character, I cannot receive the credit due to either. I wish to go to a country where I shall be estimated by my merits and not by my complexion, and I feel bound to labor for my suffering race."

Before leaving Richmond, he and Collin Teage were ordained as regular Baptist Ministers, and a little Church was organized, consisting of Lott Carey and wife, Collin Teage and wife, Joseph Langford, Colston Warring of Petersburg, Va., and Joseph Lewis, of Richmond, Va. A farewell meeting was given by the Missionary Society, at which time Carey preached his farewell sermon from Rom. 8:32. He said, in part, "I long to preach to the poor Africans the way of life and salvation. I do not know what may befall me, whether I may find a grave in the ocean, or among the savage men, or more savage wild beasts on the coasts of Africa; nor am I anxious what may become of me. I feel it my duty to go, and I very much fear that many of those who preach the Gospel in this country will blush when the Saviour calls them to give an account of their labors in His cause and tells them 'I commanded you to go into all the world and preach the Gospel to every creature.'" And with thrilling emphasis, looking around upon his audience, exclaimed, "The Saviour may ask, 'Where have you been? What have you been doing? Have you been endeavoring from the uttermost of your ability to fulfill the command I gave you? Or have you sought your own gratification and your own ease, regardless of my commands?'" The parting scene at Richmond was very affecting.

Lott Carey Sails

Various circumstances arose to prevent his sailing with the first steamer, but, with a party of thirty-eight, he and Collin Teage sailed on the Nautilus on January 23, 1821. It is further said of him, "Carey united dignity with tenderness, and manifested the spirit of one who was to become a Missionary of the cross. There was a moral sublimity in the spectacle, for he was actually making a sacrifice of all his worldly interests and was prepared for death as well as life."

At Sierra Leone

They reached their destination within forty-four days. Captain Blair treated his passengers with kindness and attention. When they reached Sierra Leone, the Colony had not yet secured a place for settlement. They could go on shore, but they had to lodge and keep their little cargo on board of the ship for four months. During this time their food exhausted. Lott Carey was compelled to go on shore to seek employment to earn his daily bread. Finding nothing in the town to do, he turned cooper and made washtubs and water buckets and sold them in Freetown Sierra Leone to keep his family from starvation. In spite of all his striving, his second wife departed for the better land. This was a sore bereavement in a strange land. Yet he had the satisfaction of knowing that she departed in the exercise of a lively faith and an assured hope of an everlasting life.

But he was not unmindful of the great object of his mission. He not only preached as he had opportunity, but established a mission for the Mandingoes at Freetown Sierra Leone.

In 1822 he removed his family to Cape Mesurado, and became one of the most active and influential members of that little community. The native tribes, repenting of the sale of the lands on the Cape, meditated the destruction of the Colony; and, after Ashmun, its salvation was not due to any one so much as Lott Carey. Mr. Ashmun has this to say of Carey: ''On his arrival in Africa, he saw before him a wide and interesting field, demanding various and energetic talents and the most devoted piety. His intellectual ability, firmness of purpose, unbending integrity, correct judgment, and disinterested benevolence, soon placed him in a conspicuous station and gave him wide and commanding influence. Though naturally diffident and retiring, his worth was too evident to allow him to continue in obscurity. It is well known that great difficulties were encountered in founding a settlement at Cape Mesurado. So appalling were the circumstances of the first settlers that soon after they had taken possession of the Cape it was proposed that they should remove to Sierra Leone. The resolution of Mr. Carey was not to be shaken; he determined to stay, and his decision had great effect in persuading others to imitate his example.''

''Carey, in one of his letters, compares the little, exposed company at Mesurado at that time to the Jews, who in rebuilding their city grasped a weapon in one hand while they labored with the other, but adds emphatically, 'There never has been an hour nor a minute, not even when the balls were flying around my head, when I could wish myself again in America.' ''

''Lott Carey, though much occupied with the affairs of the Colony and its defense, and with the practice of medicine, yet did not neglect the main object of his mission. He not only labored to promote the spiritual interest of the Church at Monrovia, but gave instructions in the rudiments of the Gospel to the Africans who had been captured from slave ships. And from letters addressed to his friends in Virginia, it appears that religion was in a flourishing condition at his Church.''

His services were especially valuable after the arrival of the Cyrus with 105 emigrants. All of these were seized with the fever, and our self-instructed Physician had his hands full; and what greatly enhanced the value of his services, they were gratuitously bestowed on all who needed them and were willing to accept them. In this large number sick, he only lost three children.

In the midst of his labors, he found time to pay attention to agricultural improvements. In one of his letters he says,

"I have a promising little crop of rice and cassada, and have planted about one hundred and eighty coffee trees this week, a part of which I expect will produce next season, as they are now in bloom. I think, sir, that in a few years we shall send you coffee of a better quality than you have ever seen brought into your market. I will send you a sample at the first opportunity."

In the autumn of 1825, a request was received from the Board at Washington, that Rev. Lott Carey should pay a visit to the United States. This accorded much with his feelings. He had it at heart to confer with friends in America, especially with the Missionary Society of Richmond, Va. On this occasion, Mr. Ashmun furnished him with ample testimonials, in which his services to the Colony are duly appreciated; and a proper consideration of his medical services recommended to the Board, which, though they were rendered without fee or hope of reward, in equity, ought not to be suffered to remain without remuneration.

This visit, however, was postponed in consequence of the urgent demand for Mr. Carey's medical service, for of the late emigrants, many were sick. Mr. Ashmun himself had the uttermost confidence in his medical skill, as appears from the following testimony: "The prescription of our excellent and experienced Assistant Physician, the Rev. Lott Carey, under the blessing of Divine Providence, so far succeeded as to afford complete relief, only leaving one in a very emaciated and feeble state in the end of about the first week in July.

"Though Mr. Carey had declined all offices which would be likely to interfere with his ministerial and missionary labors, yet so high was the estimation in which he was held, that in September, 1826, he was elected to fill the office of Vice-Agent. Indeed, all eyes were turned to him as the most fit person to fill that responsible office. His intrepidity, foresight, prudence and firmness eminently qualified him to sustain the Government and secure the welfare of the people. 'In his good sense,' says Mr. Gurley, 'moral worth, public spirit, courage, resolution and decision, the Colonial Agent had perfect confidence.'

"After securing the necessary books and finding a suitable teacher, he went to Cape Mount to prosecute his long-contemplated school at that place; and after a palaver, the King and his Chiefs unanimously gave their consent to the proposed institution. While there, he embraced the opportunity of preaching to the natives, through an interpreter.

"In one of his letters to the Richmond Missionary Society, he urges them 'to be strong in the Lord and in the power of His might, for it seems· as if the great flood gate is about to be opened upon this part of Africa. One missionary arrived here in the Ontaria, and he informs me that there are four following after him. He is all the way from Germany or Switzerland, of the Lutheran denomination. I do not know what to say, but I must say O American Christians! Look this way! come this way! and help! If you cannot come, send help for the Lord's sake. Help Africa's sons out of the devil's bush into the kingdom of God. The harvest is already white. The heathen in our vicinity are very anxious for the means of light. They will buy it, beg it, and sooner than miss it, will steal it.' Lott Carey established the school and put Rev. John Revey in charge of it—a Baptist minister—in 1825. Rev. Lott Carey opened the district of Cape Mount to the gospel of Christ.

"Upon Mr. Ashmun's departure, 1828, the whole government of the colony devolved upon Lott Carey. Mr. Ashmun's confidence in his wisdom and integrity may be learned from Mr. Ashmun's letter to the Board. 'I was enabled to arrange the concerns of the colony with Mr. Carey, even to the minutest particulars, and I have the greatest confidence that his administration will prove satisfactory to the highest degree to the Board and advantageous to the Colony.'

"Mr. Carey now called together the principal officers of the Colony and read to them, without reserve, the instructions left him by Mr. Ashmun, and requested their co-operation. 'I trust,' said he, 'through the great blessing of the Ruler of events, we shall be able to realize all the expectations of Mr. Ashmun and render entire satisfaction to the Board of Managers, if they can reconcile themselves to the necessary expense.' "

Lott Carey as a Business Man

It will give some knowledge of Lott Carey's business talents, as well as of his enterprise and patriotism, to exhibit the following deed, which was executed to him, as Agent of the Colony, by several of the Kings of the Country:

"Know all men by these presents: That we, Old King Peter, and King Governor, King James and King Long Peter, do, on this fourth day of April, in the year of our Lord, one thousand, eight hundred and twenty-eight, grant unto Lott Carey, Acting Agent of the Colony of Liberia, in behalf of the American Colonization Society, to-wit: All that tract of land on the north side of the St. Paul River, beginning at King James' line below the establishment called the Millsburg Settlement; and we, the Kings, as aforesaid, do bargain, sell, and grant unto the said Lott Carey, acting in behalf of the American Colonization Society, all the aforesaid, situated and bounded as follows: by the St. Paul River on the south, and thence running an east-northeast direction along the St. Paul River as far as he, the said Lott Carey, or his successor in the Agency, or civil authority of the Colony of Liberia, shall think proper to take up and occupy; and bounded on the west by King Jemmy's, and running thence to a northeast direction as far as our power or influence extends. We do, on this day and date, grant, as aforesaid, for the consideration, etc. The articles here omitted, and will ever defend the same against all claims whatever.

"In witness whereof, we set our hands and names:

"OLD X KING PETER.
LONG X KING PETER.
KING X GOVERNER.
KING X JAMES.

"Signed in presence of:

"ELIJAH JOHNSON.
FREDERICK JAMES.
DANIEL GEORGE."

So well did Lott Carey conduct the affairs of the Colony that had been entrusted to him that he won the commendation of every one. He visited the settlements of Caldwell and Millsburg, and took much interest in their development. He felt compelled to assist them with food until their crops were ready to harvest.

Slaver and Firmness

Towards the close of June, the whole colony was thrown into excitement. Three suspicious vessels put into harbor. One anchored within reach of the Fort guns. Lott Carey waited long for the ship to put up her flag or send her boat ashore and make known her errand, but she failed to do so. Then he fired a shot near her. She hastened to put up the Spanish flag and send one of her boats ashore to say that she was not a slaver, but had come to get wood and water. Carey replied that he did not believe a word of it and that if they were not gone within an hour he would fire upon them. They lost no time to weigh anchor and move out.

He recommended to the Board the purchase of a coastwise schooner that could run as far as Cape Palmas. He also advised the Board of Managers to obtain a strip of ground between Bassa Cove and a place called Sesters, that the Colonists might come in possession of the entire coast.

Sad and Lamentable Death of Lott Carey

The slave trade was one of the biggest enemies that the Colonist had to meet. While they dared not, in their helpless condition, go out of their territory to do anything against it, yet they felt duty-bound to defend the Colony.

The Government had established a post at a place called Digby, not far distant from Monrovia. Here they had a government house for the storing of goods to supply the surrounding settlement.

The natives of the district were in league with the slavers. The natives of Africa get their living by selling one another. Domestic slavery in Africa among the Africans themselves is far worse and inhuman than ever it was in the United States. All of this was displeasing to Lott Carey. He remonstrated with the natives and tried over and over again to adjust the matter amicably, but in vain. He sent a letter to the slaver, which was intercepted by the natives and destroyed. They ventured further than this: they even took possession of the house for their business of slave-trading. Carey demanded that they give up the property, but they laughed him to scorn. Therefore, there could be nothing done to bring the law into force against the intruder. Accordingly, Lott Carey ordered out two companies of the militia to reckon with the offenders at Digby. And while he and several others were in the magazine manufacturing cartridges to be used in that expedition, a candle was upset, igniting the loose powder, which at once caused an explosion of the magazine. This terrible accident caused the

untimely death of this great hero. "When his sun had
risen to its meridian, it was suddenly smitten out without
a moment's warning." How sad! What calamity to the
infant Colony! One, in commenting upon his death and
the honor that was due him as a pioneer in that glorious
undertaking of founding a Republic on the West Coast of
Africa, has said:

> Shall none record the honored name
>   Of Afric's favored son?
> Or twine the deathless wreath of fame
>   For him whose race is run?
> While angels crown the saint above,
> Has earth no voice to own her love?
>
> Where'er the Patriot rests his head,
>   A stately pile appears,
> While warriors sleep on glory's bed
>   Beneath a nation's tears.
> And shall no tribute rise to thee,
> Thou fearless friend of liberty?
>
> Yes, Afric's sunny skies have gleamed
>   On many a scene sublime,
> But more than hope has ever dreamed
>   Is destined for that clime.
> The chains shall burst, the slaves be free,
> And millions bless thy memory.
>
> Thy need shall be a nation's love,
>   Thy praise the free man's song,
> And in thy star-wreathed home above,
>   Thou mayst the theme prolong:
> For hymns of praise from Afric's plain
> Shall mingle with seraphic strains.

Careysburg Established

About six weeks after the sad demise of Rev. Lott Carey,
Dr. Randall arrived, December 22, 1828. Dr. Mechlin, who
had been appointed Physician for the Colony, accompanied

him. They were favorably surprised at the beautiful appearance of the village, Monrovia.

One of Dr. Randall's first duties was to find a suitable location for some recaptured African slaves. Lott Carey had purchased some territory about fifty miles southeast of Monrovia, and upon this the captured natives were located and the place named in honor of Lott Carey—"Carystown," now Careysburg.

Dr. Randall, in visiting King Boatswain and exploring the upper St. Paul River, caught a cold, from which he could not be relieved and the end soon came. Dr. Mecklin, who was sent out as Physician of the Colony, took his place. Needing more territory, he made a trip to Bassa and bought a tract of land near the mouth of St. John River. This had long been a coveted spot also. Many inducements were offered for settlers to go to this district, and at once thirty strong men with their families volunteered to go.

Four towns were now established, namely: Monrovia, Caldwell, Millsburg—named for Mills and Burges—and Bassa Cove. Maryland Colonization Society sent out a Colony to the Cape Palmas District, known as Maryland. This Colony remained separate and distinct from the other Colonies until the Independence of Liberia. Robertsport, or Capt Mount District, was established, and Liberia reached its limit upon the coastwise boundary.

CHAPTER VI

The Country and Its Inhabitants

The Republic of Liberia is situated upon the West Coast of Africa and lies between latitude 4 degrees, 41 minutes, and 6 degrees, 48 minutes north, and between longitude 8 degrees and 8 minutes, and 11 degrees and 20 minutes west. It is bounded on the east by the French, on the south by the Cavalla River, one the west by the Atlantic Ocean, and on the north by the Mannah River.

Topography

There are foothills all along the coast, but no high mountains. Near the beach, the land, for the most part, is sandy loam and well wooded. Farther back, the hinterland is more rugged and hilly. The Mandingo Plateau, near the boundary, is one of the highest elevations in Liberia. All of Liberia is well wooded, and numerous creeks and rivers water the country.

Geography

Mannah River. This is the boundary between Liberia and the English possessions on the north, and it is about six miles southeast of Sulyma River.

The Sugari and Marphy Rivers are in the vicinity of Cape Mount. These rivers, with Fisherman Lake, have a common outlet, across which the surf breaks heavily. The former river extends five and one-half miles in a northernly and southernly direction.

Half Cape Mount River. About half-way between Cape Mount and Mesurado is a little stream, but in the dry season it is quite closed by a sandbar.

Po River. This is a small stream eight miles southeast of the Cape Mount River.

St. Paul River. This is the most important river in Liberia. It is almost a mile wide in the Virginia District and extends for twenty-five miles to the Rapids. It was navigated by Mr. Randall, who found it far up beyond the Rapids a large river like the Amazon. It takes its rise from the Mandingo Plateau and empties into the Atlantic Ocean.

Mesurado River. This is a large river, which flows around the Cape. It rises from the hills in the east and flows into the Atlantic Ocean.

Junk River. This is also a large river and forms the boundary line between Bassa and Mesurado Counties.

Little Bassa River. This river is situated within one mile of Marshall Point, southeast.

Grand Bassa River. This river is made up of three branches—St. John, central, and Mecklin on one side, and Benson on the other. They empty by one mouth in the Atlantic.

Little Kulloh River. It lies four miles southeast of Trade Town, and is accessible to small boats.

Tembo River. It is situated three miles southeast of Grand Kollah Vlilage. Half a mile north of Tembo it is known as Tembo River.

Between Tembo River and Grand Sestos are two small streams called Fen and Manna.

On the coast, between Cestos Point and Rock Cess Point, flow two small rivers known as Pua and Pobamo.

New River. This is a small river that enters the sea at Rock Cess Point.

Bruni River. Two miles south of the New River is the Bruni.

Sanguin River. The Sanguin River empties into Baffu Bay, above Greenville and Sinoe.

Tubo River. Between Tassu Point and the next point of land to the southward is Tubo River.

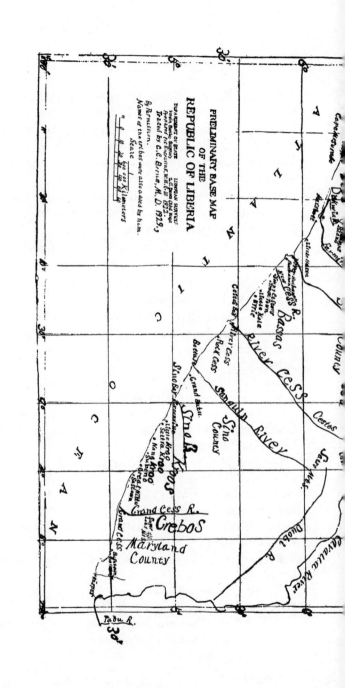

PRELIMINARY BASE MAP
OF THE
REPUBLIC OF LIBERIA

DEPARTMENT OF STATE
LIBERIAN SURVEY
Traced by O. C. Brune, M. D. 1929.
By Permission.
Names of the tribes were also added by him.

Scale

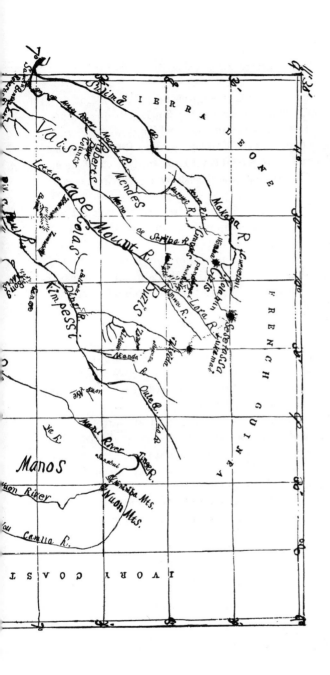

Baffni River. This branch empties near Baffu Point.

Sinoe River. This is a large river, flowing through Sinoe County. There are three channels by which boats may enter this river—between North Point and Allen Rocks, between Allen Rocks and a large oval sand bank to the east of them, and between the sand bank and Fishtown. The first is said to be the best.

Between Blubarra Point and Settra Cru there is a long, narrow lagoon which is supplied by two rivers, the Bluba and Plassa.

Uno River. The western mouth of Uno River is situated three and one-half miles from King Wells Point, southeast; the eastern branch empties into the sea three miles east of the western branch.

Dru River. Two miles southeast of Great Niffu is Dru River.

Ersereus River. Southeast upon the coast for two and one-half miles from Dru River you reach Ersereus River.

Grand Cesters River. About one mile east of Cesters Point is the Grand Cesters River.

Garaway River empties into the ocean at Garaway.

Jida, Dia, Mnao Rivers. In the eight miles distance between Garaway and Fish Town you find these three rivers.

Hoffman River. This enters the ocean on the northeast side of the Cape Palmas Peninsula.

Cavalla River. This is a boundary between Liberian and French possessions, and is navigable for small steamers for fifty miles.

Feruma River is near Sasstown.

Mountains of Liberia

Tokowelle. In the District of Bopora.

Wula. On longitude 7 degrees and between latitude 7 and 30 degrees.

Bong. On longitude 7 degrees and latitude 10 degrees.

Nuon. North latitude 30 degrees, and south latitude 30 degrees.

Satro. On longitude 6 degrees and latitude 30 degrees, south.

Islands

The most important island is called Bushrod, in honor of Mr. Bushrod Washington, the first President of the Colonization Society. It is just across the river from Monrovia and is surrounded by the Atlantic Ocean, Stockton Creek, and the St. Paul River. It is about eight miles long and three miles wide.

Perseverance Island. This lies beside Cape Mesurado, at the mouth of the Mesurado River. Here the Colonists landed and remained from January 9th until April 25, 1822.

Russworm Island. So named for Governor Russworm, first Governor of Maryland Colony. It lies near the main land of Cape Palmas. It is 720 yards long and 120 broad. It is sometimes called "Dead Man's Island," because the original inhabitants buried their dead there.

Lakes

Shepard Lake. This is a very beautiful lake in Robertsport County, near Cape Mount. It is ten miles long and six miles wide and is filled with the finest fish in the world.

Benson Lake. This lake is situated in the District of Cape Palmas. It was named for President Benson. It runs parallel with the ocean. Its dimensions are about the same as Shepard Lake.

Capes

There are three Capes upon the coast of Liberia. Cape Palmas, the southern extremity of the country, near the Cavalla River; Cape Mesurado, upon which Monrovia is situated, and Cape Mount, at Grand Cape Mount, upon the northwest boundary.

The People

The people of Liberia are of four classes, namely: Americo-Liberians are those who came from America, or their children, and they are the ruling class; civilized natives; recaptured Africans, known as Congoes; and the Aborigines, the original inhabitants.

The civilized natives are those who have been brought up in the homes of the Americo-Liberians and are thenceforth participants in the affairs of the State.

The Congoes are those who were captured upon the high seas, and instead of being taken back to Congo after the founding of the Republic, for convenience were landed in Liberia. In an effort to break up the slave trade, these were captured from slaving ships by English and American men-o'-war.

The original inhabitants consists of many native tribes. They are estimated at 2,000,000. The most conspicuous tribes are:

The Cru. These are the navigators and sailors. They delight to pull the row boats over the boisterous surf. The white men are no sailors to compare with them. When the big ships reach the coast of Africa, the white stevedores and crew retire and give the ship over to the Cru men. They go upon the bridge as pilots and take all the machines in charge, as well as the cargo. The Spaniards take charge of the ship when it reaches the Spanish Islands, but the Spanish stevedores are not to be compared with the Cru men in dexterity. I said to one of the officers once while at the islands, "Why do you not hurry these Spaniards as you did the Cru boys." They replied, "It will do no good." I could write a separate book upon what I have seen the Cru boys do with row boats upon the coast.

While traveling from Congo to Liberia upon the Ville de Anverse, we stopped at Libreville, on the Gaboon River, to load mahogany logs. The wind was blowing a rapid gale, the waves were rolling hundreds of feet up the beach. The captain contended that he must send on shore for those logs, storm or no storm. The white seamen said that they would see him in torment before they would go ashore with that boat. But you should have heard the Cru boys singing and seen them bringing the timber on board!

Once while looking through our field glasses at the row boat that had gone ashore, we beheld, and lo! every one of the poor boys was out of the boat into the fitful deep. As heartless as the old captain was, he turned around to me with a shudder and said, "One of my boys is gone this time." The next second he looked and shouted, "No, there they all are; those boys are a miracle!" When they did manage to return to the ship, one boy had his forearm fractured in two places, and another had his ear torn from his head. The captain had long since, when I first went on board, made me ship doctor. The boy with the fractured limb, we were compelled to leave in the hospital at Sierra Leone because the ship did not have any plaster paris. The Cru people are great swimmers. They cannot be easily drowned.

There is an interesting tradition about the Cru boys. The Cru people say it is true. At a place down the coast called Nana Cru, when a Cru boy is two years old he must stand the Cru test in this manner: All of his people take him out to the beach, with a big crowd of admirers and many sight-seers. The boy to be tested is greased well in palm oil. They have no trouble to undress him, for he has never worn more than a string of beads about his waist. They go through the Cru ceremony, recalling the many noble deeds of his ancestors, how they were thrown overboard and swam ashore, how some of them remained a whole night in the ocean upon a paddle, etc. Then the strongest man in the midst takes the little boy and throws him out as far as he can in the great Atlantic Ocean. He must swim or drown. If he is pure Cru, they say he will swim. If he swims, then they rush in and rescue him with a great shout, and he is carried back to the town with loud rejoicing.

The Crus are industrious, great farmers and fishermen. They go fishing in the ocean in little " dug outs"—a boat dug out of a tree. The Cru people are apt to learn, kind and obliging.

The Vey. The Vey are modest and sincere people. They occupy the northwestern section of the Republic. They are for the most part quiet and peaceful. They have a language all their own. They are the only people whom I know in Liberia who originated an alphabet for their language. Lott Carey opened the Vey country in 1825 and placed a teacher out there. This teacher taught through an interpreter. The interpreter became so interested in his own language that he dreamed how he might make figures to represent the sounds of the letters. He arose from sleep and cut out the figures according to his dream, and he had invented characters to write his language. You shall know his name—it is Dwala Bukere. Many of the Vey people can write very fluently in their language.

They are industrial people. The men make cloth; weave it upon their own looms. They are smaller than our looms in America, but follow the same principle. The women farm, make pottery and fish. Their religion is mostly Mohamedan. They believe in polygamy and slavery.

Many of their people have risen to prominence and honor in the Republic. Mr. Sandy Roberts was a noted architect and builder. Mr. Momolu Massaquoir is Consul-General in Germany for Liberia, and Counselor Beselow is Associate Justice of the Supreme Court.

The Gola. The Gola people are more war-like than most of the other tribes. They have a checkered history. They are much improved in 1926. They have put up their weapons and are now entering the Churches and begging for schools. They occupy the Northern Section.

Pessie. The Pessie people are the laborers of the Republic. They are verily the "hewers of wood and drawers of water." In time, they will own the soil and be independent people. They are congenial and are fast becoming Christians.

Mendi and Booze. The Mendi and Booze are interior tribes and are yet in the "valley and shadow of death." They engage in agriculture and make the soldiers of the Republic.

The Grebo Tribe. These people inhabit the Southwestern Territory. They are naturally intelligent. In the matter of culture and erudition, they easily excell all the other tribes. I saw one boy, said to be a Grebo boy, win five prizes in a commencement exercise in the West African College at Monrovia. Hon. Too Westly was vice-president with President King during his second term.

The Mandingo Tribe. They occupy the Mandingo Plateau, far back upon the eastern boundary. They are a mixed race, partly Moor or Arab. They speak several languages. They write in Arabic characters. They weave pretty cloth, and do very excellent bead work. They manufacture knives, spears and hoes from the crude iron ore. They also make arrow-heads of steel.

The Bassa people. They are not generally liked in Liberia, because they are said to be "medicine men," who can work "tricks," put you to sleep and rob your house. Whether they can actually do all the people say they can or no, I wish to relate an experience that I had with them.

One day my house boy ran away, and I had no one to

work for me. In the morning, some Bassa boys were passing and I asked them if they wished to work. They replied in the affirmative. I employed them to go to the woods and cut me some wood. I did not own any wood land, but the custom in Africa is that you can cut wood upon any one's land as long as the owner does not object. Dead trees are always given away.

I gave the three of them cutlasses and they marched off towards the jungle. In a reasonable time they returned with splendid bundles of fire wood. Then I said to them, "Now, you are hungry and want to eat." They said, "Yes." I gave them rice and fish and they proceeded to make the fire and prepare the food. Upon the second thought, I went back into the cook house (we keep the cook house detached from the regular dwelling on account of fire.) There are no fire companies in Africa. I asked them if they would also cook some food for me. They agreed. While the food was cooking, I was constantly going back and forth, watching to see what was going on. Presently I saw one of the men (the one that had the black mark running from the top of his forehead down to the tip end of his nose) indicating, according to their tribal marks, a high medicine man, scraping some bark from a stick that he had brought from the woods. I said to him, "What is that, medicine?" He answered in a jocular mood, "Yes." Then I prevailed upon him to give me over his medicine until my food was done, which he did, very reluctantly. I assured him, however, that when my food was done he could have all of his medicine back. I was sharp, but not sharp enough, for I truly believe that he had put some of that bark or some other thing in my food. I will complete my story and let you draw conclusions.

When they had eaten their food and I had given them a "dash" on top, I asked if any of them desired to remain with me for the night? To my surprise, the medicine man was the very one to consent. Later in the afternoon, a friend of mine passed that way and saw the Bassa man in my house. She stopped and asked me what was I doing with that Bassa medicine man in my house? She asked me also if he would sleep there at night; if so, where would I put him? I showed her the shed room where all of my boys usually slept. She begged me not to let him sleep there, but to put him out into the cook house; for, said she, ''If you allow that man to sleep in your house with you, he will wake up in the night and put you to sleep and take everything in your house.''

I took her advice and put his bed out into the kitchen and locked my door securely. The next morning, the day broke as usual. I looked around in my house in a drowsy mood. Every thing seemed to be there, but I was profoundly sleepy. I did not have energy enough to dress myself. I took my steamer chair and hobbled out under the shade of a plum tree in the yard, and there I stretched myself out in my pajamas, just as I had slept during the night.

My mind tried to reason with me, ''You are a medical doctor; suppose some one should come for treatment and catch you out here in your night clothes?'' I replied, ''I cannot help it, I must sleep.'' The Bassa man came and told me he was going. I told him to go, and kept on sleeping. I sat there and slept without food and clothing until 2 o'clock in the day. The natives said, to have completed the anesthetic, he would powder the bark and sprinkle the dust in my face while asleep. It is so warm, we always perspire greatly in our sleep in Africa, so there would be no difficulty in absorbing the dust into the pores of the skin. And as sleepy as I was, I do not doubt it in the least. I intended to have made some tests of the bark.

The Bassa Tribe, however, has obtained the highest dis-

Dr. C. C. Boone Teaching the Natives

A Congo House

tinction of any of the tribes of the Republic. Dr. B. W. Payne, the Secretary of Education and a member of the Cabinet, is a graduate of the Meherry Medical School of the United States. The Hon. B. Cheeseman, a pure Bassa man, born at Idina, was President of the Country.

Recaptured Africans

They consist almost entirely of people from the Congo basin of Central Africa. When these poor people were rescued upon the high seas from the slave ships, instead of taking them back to their homes in the Congo, they were dumped into Liberia. But notwithstanding they had no advantage of civilization, they compare favorably with the Americao-Liberians in their settlements, farms, manners and Christianity. They have entered gladly into the Republic and have helped to fight some of Liberia's hardest battles with the Aboriginal tribes.

Habits and Customs of the Liberian People

This is perhaps the most delicate subject of the whole book. It is perplexing because of its heterogeneous character. The subject is manifold and interstitial in composition, and so interwoven with civilization on the one hand and heathenism on the other that it is exceedingly difficult to discuss and be judged fair to all sides and phases involved.

Mixture of Clans and Habits

The civilized Liberian, to maintain his standing as a light and a ruler of the country, must live in some way aloof from the people he governs. This is the custom in America, and it is far more necessary in Africa. The civilized class is, however, principally dependent upon the Aboriginal class for servants; consequently, the natives in the interior find their way down to the Cape, upon the coast, and into the different settlements looking for work, and in this way drift into the homes of the Americo-Liberians. It may happen that he enters a home where he may be cruelly treated at first, and the casual observer may think that he is being held as a slave   Nevertheless, this is the hard way that so many native boys in Liberia have risen from idolaters to believers in Jesus Christ and honorable participants in the Liberian Government, that one has to take time to work out these intricate problems before spreading his opinion to the world.

Many times the casual observer is chagrined by mirage of ignorance that makes things, upon first sight, look differently from what they are. I never will forget my first trip across the ocean, when I was making my debut in mission work twenty-five years ago. There was a native African boy on board, and he was constantly in association with a white man whom he addressed as "Master." Such an encomium was such a reminder of the horrors of by-gone days that it was annoying to us who had been free-born or of Indian descent. Therefore, I could not be contented until I had made some persistent inquiries concerning that boy and his companion.

This is the information that I gained. The white man had taken the boy from the African bush and carried him to America, educated him and was then taking him back to Africa at his own—the white man's—expense. Suppose I had gotten up the first time I heard that salutation and insulted that white man? Then I would have been disgraced throughout the entire trip. In a similar way, upon the spur of the moment, many visitors going into Africa have gotten the wrong conception of affairs and have grossly misjudged and miscalculated missionary enterprises.

Therefore, the Liberian coming in contact with the African boys and people have to cautionsly watch the character of the person he has under his control and administer to him as his ability to reciprocate is manifested. In many instances, the native boy may be forced, when he first enters the home, to carry the books of the civilized children to school, then return to cut grass in the yard until the school is out, when he must return and bring the books back for the children. If a person just arriving in the country sees this, he may remark, "That is a shame"! But the visitor does not know that if that African boy is taken from the hinterland and placed at once into school with strange children that he will remain in civilization for only a short time; he would run away overnight. When I first went to Africa, I had many such occurrences. We would take the raw native boys, give them a new suit of clothes, send them down to the water to bathe and comb their hair. Then they were carried into the school. The very next day they could not be found. I did that a half-dozen times until at last I said to my wife, "We will give no other boy clothes until he has worked long enough to pay for them." This worked like a charm. We made the next boy remain in dirt and rags for three months before we presented him a suit of clothes, and he remained with me for three years.

When the native boy gets used to civilization, then he is inducted into the home circle and shares all the benefits of civilization and Christianity. This is, in a concrete way, the problems of the civilized Liberian.

Partaking of Native Language and Customs

In this contact referred to above, there is a constant stimulus which eminates from the civilized man to the native, and there is also an incessant struggle by the civilized man to overcome the inertia of the native habit. In daily contact with the heathen natives, one must fight to keep above the native tide of polygamy, witchcraft and moral lethargy.

Polygamy

It is not easy for us who have been brought up under Christian influences to understand the intricate and vexing question of polygamy. When our wife is sick, we delight to do what we can to spare her and relieve her as much as possible from the burdens of the home. But not so with the African man. If he is caught cooking, washing or sweeping the house and taking the woman's work, he is ridiculed, scorned and ignored. The polygamist, when one wife is sick or disabled in any way, the next wife in turn must take up her duties and keep up the continuity of the home.

When a woman becomes a mother, she (according to African custom) is practically divorced from connubial obligations until she has weaned the child. The laws of Liberia countenance polygamy, and all the natives practice it. The civilized are permitted to have housekeepers, so that the Church has a tremendous effort to maintain the standard of monogamy.

Slavery

All the natives of Africa traffic in slavery. The Liberian laws forbid slavery, and any one reported is severely punished if found guilty. When, however, that person dealing in the slave trade has to furnish your vegetables and supply your table with food from his farm, it causes meditation before attempting to break up his home.

Colonial Governments

Liberia, like all the other Colonial Governments in Africa, permits the natives to conduct their own affairs in their own way as they have been doing from time immemorial. It is also the custom now to appoint certain chiefs to act as Government officers and hear matters and try cases for their own people.

Ponds

This is a system similar to what we had in North Carolina when I was a boy. Fatherless and homeless children were bound out according to law until they were twenty-one years old. I attended school with such a boy. He had to carry all the school books for the other children, and in case of storm had to go through the rain to bring vehicle and wraps for the other members of the family.

This is about the same system in Liberia, or as near a comparison as I know, only, in many instances, it it stretched out into actual slavery. Usually a man comes to borrow $20 or $30 and leaves the child as surety until the money can be replaced. If he never comes back with the money, as is the case ninety-nine times out of the hundred, the boy is with the man who furnished the money as his own boy or servant.

This position, however, in Liberia does not prohibit the boy from becoming a citizen and partaking of all the rights of citizenship. It is, nevertheless, a very perplexing problem with which to deal.

Home Life and Morals

Grandmothers and relatives guard the morals of the young people and stringent native laws protect the adults. Thrown around these home restrictions are the "Greegree Bush" for the women and the "Devil Bush" for the boys. In these schools in which the children are kept for long periods, they are trained in the modes of self-protection and the "fine arts" interwoven into the every-day African life.

Far back in the interior, the young girls wear a small deer horn, which denotes that they have not been discharged from the girls' school. In other words, when they have completed their period of training, they are, according to native vernacular, "washed" and turned out from

the school, as in civilized circles, when they have made their
debut; then they are to be spoken to or greeted by men,
but as long as that horn is strung around them, no one must
approach them, *upon their life,* or their life will be taken.
It is not with the African, the question of a few months
upon the road or a short prison term, with a possible par-
don, but it means your head.

Courtship and Marriage.

The matter of courtship is omitted in the native life. The
matches are usually made by the older people. Love has no
part in the African matrimony. Any man may marry as
many wives as he can purchase, the price being from forty
to fifty dollars, according to the age and qualities of the
person. The civilized Liberian conducts his home life like
all civilized individuals, betrothing and marrying in the
usual style.

Fetiches

Africans, like all other people, believe in "luck." While
they do not make use of the *horse shoe* and the *rabbit foot*
as the Americans do, yet they have the same fear of some
unseen evil that constantly lurks around them. To appease
the anger of this unseen foe, they wear many charms. Some
they wear around their waist underneath all clothing, and
others they wear on their arms, necks and legs. They go so
far as to place these modes of protection in their farms to
prevent theft, and upon their houses to secure against destruction.

Spirits and Spiritism

I have found that the African people have no conception
of the soul. They believe in spirits, they believe that God
is a Spirit, and that the devil is a spirit. They also believe
in devil or evil spirits; and, as strange as these things may
seem, they prepare the mind of the heathen for the recep-

tion of Christianity or the indwelling of the Great Spirit, God. This description has reference to the Aborigines, not civilized.

Foods

The foods of the Liberians are the foods common to all Central Africa—rice, casava, sweet potatoes, eddoes, breadfruit, fish, beans, peas, string beans, okra, collard greens, cabbage, cucumbers, corn, pumpkins, squash, arrowroot and peanuts. Meat is scarce and is obtained once or twice a week. These foods are prepared in a very wholesome manner and are highly palatable, except for the large arount of red pepper that all Africans use.

Cannibalism

Much has been said about Africa and cannibalism, and some have made references to Liberia in that connection. But with my many years residence in Africa, I can not truthfully say whether such a practice really exists. Far back in the interior, the native women have laws that govern their household duties that are not to be broken by any one. And one of their special laws is that no one must lift the top of their pots when they are cooking. When that stew is done, no one can really tell just of what it is composed; we lay special emphasis upon the taste, rather than the composition.

The native men tell us that all the tribes that have sharp teeth like a dog are cannibals. As soon as the permanent teeth are grown, they are filed to a point, the enamel grows over them, and they look like the teeth of the lower animals. It is said that these teeth are used to tear the flesh instead of biting, as we do. Some of the sharp-teeth people are found in Liberia, French and Belgian Congo.

Are Other People Cannibals?

When going out to Africa, in 1901, I went on shore at

one of the Spanish islands, and what was my astonishment
when I saw in the public square a statue, at the base of
which were scattered skulls and bones! I stopped and inquired the meaning of such a statue. It was explained to
me that the people of the island once ate each other and the
monument was erected in honor of the man who came
among them and put an end to cannibalism.

The following excerpt from the "Durham Times," Durham, N. C., U. S. A., will be interesting: "Budapest, May
12.—The inhabitants or man-eating savages were discovered near the Hungarian village Raba-Puspoki by Hungarian National Museum, which find confirms the theory
of Prof. J. Baylor, director of the Vienna National History
Museum, that the valley of the Danube was populated 4,500
or 5,000 years ago with cannibals, who were, however, not
lacking a certain cultural standard. These cannibals seem
to have developed a special art in cooking, and they evidently prepared their human enemies with great care and
epicurean subtlety. They used a considerable number of
cooking utensils for roasting, frying, and boiling their prisoners whom they turned to appetizing meals, as it is shown
by the human bones contained in the clay and stone vessels."

Dress

The Africans dress to suit the times. Every day, for
working in the field, the women wear a cloth around their
loins. When hunting, the men are also scantily dressed.
All of these people have an extra touch for special occa-
sions. At a ball, wedding or funeral, you will be surprised
to see the same woman who was working in the field on yes-
terday in her loin cloth now neatly costumed in her velvet
"toga." The civilized Americo-Liberian dresses just like
the American Negro, only more carefully and primly. America being far away, the Liberians partake of the German and

English manners and customs, in some respects, more than the American.

Games

The Liberians have many games, which they play with much enthusiasm. The Cru boys play hiding pennies in the sand upon the beach and finding them by throwing a long nail through the sand. The girls engage in many different ring plays, while the "big 'Merica" man plays checkers, cards, and all the games of the elite society.

Climate

The climate is favorable. I say it is subtropical because it is so vastly different from the climate farther down in the tropics. In Liberia, it is neither hot nor cold. Liberia seems to be wedged in between the temperate and torid zones. The temperature ranges from 65 degrees Fahrenheit to 87 degrees. It is just a mild, nice climate the entire year.

Rainfall and Seasons

When I visited Liberia in 1906, I asked a lady how often did it rain in Liberia? She replied about as often as it did in America. I was so certain that she was passing me a joke that I also passed on and left her. Now, coming to live in the country, I find her words true. In 1925 the average rainfall was estimated at 179 inches. When Rev. J. E. East, who had been a missionary in South Africa, visited Liberia he was astonished at the abundant rainfall. He remarked that the scarcity of rain in South Africa was a great agricultural hindrance.

I have never seen that two authors agreed in the description of the climate. All parties you ask about the seasons here differ. The truth of the whole matter is this: the climate today in Liberia is not like it was thirty years ago. According to Rev. J. O. Hayes and many of the older citizens, the rainy season is not as severe now as it once was.

As I have observed it, scrutinizingly, for twelve years, it is briefly this: the dry season begins in November and continues through February. There may be occasional showers in November and February, but December and January are perfectly dry.

On that account, all of the annual meetings are planned in December and the Legislature also assembles at that time. The rains begin in March and steadily increase until the latter portion of June. There is a short period, beginning about the middle of July and continuing until the end of the month, called the "middle dry." In August the rains begin again and continue until towards the last of November. It is a puzzle to know in which month the rains are most abundant. Some years, June has more rain, and others September has the greatest downpour. There can be no set rule as to which month is the more rain, for the seasons vary.

Heat and Cold

In Liberia, the cool season is during the rains. Just before the real beginning of the rains in Mrach, the weather is hottest of the whole year.

Hamatan Winds

In the month of December there comes upon the Liberian coast a very searching wind from the Northwest. It is cool, but tends to produce a feeling akin to hay fever.

Industries and Products

Coffee. Coffee is cultivated; it does not grow wild in the forest to be gathered *ad libitum*. The tree grows from ten to fifteen feet in height. The coffee berry grows in a pod, usually four grains to the pod. When the berry is red and ripe, it is picked off and put out in the sun to dry. In Africa, it only takes four or five days to dry it. Then it is ground in a machine or beaten in a mortar and the hull removed. Still the grain is enclosed in a thin, closely fitting membrane or sheath. To remove this it must again be carried through the mortar or machine. Now the cleaned grains must be separated from the chaff; therefore it must be fanned and picked. Liberia is sadly in need of a machine to do this work.

Rubber. Rubber is found in the forest in vines, and rubber trees are also cultivated. The bark of the rubber tree resembles the maple, and the tree attains the height of from forty to sixty feet. The rubber is obtained by tapping the tree or scraping away a section of the bark in the form of a triangle. At the apex of the triangle a cup is placed to catch the latex that resembles milk in its appearance. This is dried and then beaten until it is ready for shipment. (See treatise under Firestone Rubber Company.)

Ivory. Ivory is obtained from the tusk of the elephant. It is not very plentiful in Liberia because the elephants are pigmies and do not furnish large tusks. Beads, napkin-rings, handles for walking-canes and many useful things are made of it.

Sugar Cane. The soil and climate of Liberia are very suitable for the growth of the sugar cane. It was cultivated by the early settlers extensively. The yield is abundant. So profitable was the industry that the Liberians not only supplied the home market, but shipped sugar to the United States. The firm of Yates & Poterfield had a line of schooners that plyed between Liberia and America, trading in sugar, palm oil, ginger, hides, etc.

Fruits and Products of the Forest.

Limes, sweet and sour lemons, oranges, pineapples, pomegranates, pawpaws, soursaps, sweetsaps, many species of bananas, plantains, grapes and grapefruit, cocoa, cocoanuts, mango plums, golden plums, breadfruit, alligator pears and watermelons abound.

Products that grow wild. Palm nuts, cola nuts, walnuts, cherries, troves, Christmas berries, and what the Liberian calls "peaches."

Food and Vegetables that Deserve Special Mention

Palm oil is produced from the palm nuts. These grow upon high trees. They always grow in bunches about the top. One bunch may contain three hundred palm nuts. The raw palm nuts are sold at the market ten for one cent.

The oil is obtained by first heating the nuts in hot water. Then they are placed in a mortar and beaten. In this way the pulp is removed from the nut itself. The pulp and fiber are then boiled again. This removes all the oil that may cling to the fibers. The mixture is then washed and all the fiber removed. Much water is added and the pulp is now thoroughly boiled and the oil floats upon the top and is skimmed off. Further refining makes it white almost like American lard. The palm butter that is left is very good for seasoning beans, peas, etc.

Pawpaws I have styled our African cantaloupe. It grows upon a tree, but looks just like a cantaloupe. It is yellow inside and much sweeter than a cantaloupe. The seeds are said to contain pepsin.

Soursaps and Sweetsaps grow upon trees and are covered with prickly green skin. Inside, the meat is white, containing black seeds. The fruit is made up in layers. When you take out a part of the fruit and press upon it, a beautiful white juice exudes from it. This is what I have called our African ice cream. It is very delicious.

Colanuts grow upon high trees that resemble the oak. They may be several in a pod. They are said to contain cocaine. They are very energizing. The native carriers can march for hours wagging their heavy loads if they can get colanuts to chew as they march.

Watermelons grow well in Liberia. I grew six nice ones in my little garden at Monrovia. They flourish at a place named Roysville (for President Roye). Because the Roys-ville people live upon the sand beach, they almost have a monopoly of that particular industry.

Breadfruit grows upon large green trees and is round. In size, it is a little larger than the cocoanut. When fully ripe it is very good and resembles the Irish potato in appearance and taste.

The yam has no resemblance to the American potato called "yam." It is grown from cuttings like a white potato. Sometimes if you plant the cutting around a dead tree they will grow and meet all around the tree in one solid potato. I once grew one like that and had to sever it into parts to get it from around the tree. It weighed seventy-five pounds.

Native Foods of Interest

Dum Boy. This is a special dish of the Liberians, made by cooking the casava and beating it in the mortar until it is tough and elastic. It is then taken out and eaten with soup by the spoonful. And the trick is, you must not chew it. I just had to chew what I ate, to the hilarity of the Liberians.

Palaversas. This is a mixture of cooked rice and palm oil, over which is poured a fruit juice from the "bush." They say this gives the food a very good flavor. This fruit juice is like rubber, and makes the food rope like boiled sugar. It tastes pretty well, but it is hard to eat when you have donned your best clothes.

Palm Chop. This kind of food they make of palm oil, and is like our Brunswick stew. With a little piece of fresh meat thrown into it, it is very appetizing. I was fond of palm chop.

The Soil

The soil is the most fertile of the African continent. It is not difficult to have perpetual crops, one upon the hills during the rains and one in the lowlands in the dry season.

The land contains many minerals. Lott Carey testified that the men in his day smelted the iron ore and made their farming implements. I see that the early records speak of the discovery of coal. But I am sure that this was a mistake, as I have traveled and labored there for twelve years without seeing or hearing of such a thing.

Gold

Gold dust was one of the early exports from Liberia. And there is some of it left. Native men brought much of the production to me to sell and some of the gold in the crude state to test. One lady sent me a nugget to test that was all of 70 per cent gold.

Precious Stones

These are plentiful in Liberia. There are thousands of valuable quartz crystals. Once when visiting one of my deacons (I had the honor of being the pastor of the Church established by Lott Carey for eight years), he took me into a back room, and pulling out a long drawer he showed me some of the most magnificent stones that I ever saw. I asked him where he obtained such rare articles, and, laughing, he replied, "Here in Liberia."

A Trace of Oil

I was so busy as Physician and Pastor that I never had the time to search into the truthfulness of many good things about which the Liberians informed me. This, however, was an intensely interesting story. A man once told me of a pond of water in which if you threw a stick, when the stick

was removed it would burn as if it had been in kerosene oil.
Many said it was true.

Animals

The country is full of animals. But they do not come to
town. They remain in the forest, and you may live your
life in Africa and never see a wild animal. I was there,
one hundred and fifty miles in the interior, for three years
before I saw a monkey. Because you go to Africa it does
not mean that you will be attacked by wild beasts. Those
animals are very keen on human scent. And you may leave
your station and go out into the forest hunting, and then
may not see an animal unless you have some trained hunter
with you who may understand how to go against the wind,
so that the animals will not get your scent. The animals are
not as large here in Liberia as they are further south in
Africa.

You will find in Liberia elephants, leopards, hippopota-
mus, leopard cat, wild cat, boar, gnu, heart beasts, porcu-
pine, jackal, baboon, mangoose, chimpanzee, monkey, guinea
pigs, squirrels, gwana, frogs.

The Americans who are there raise such things as they
have known in America—hogs, goats, sheep, horses, cattle,
chickens, guinea fowls, ducks, turkeys and geese. They have
not yet learned to go in for stock raising and keeping dairy
farms. That is a much-needed industry in Liberia. There
are very good grazing lands.

Reptiles

The boaconstrictor still holds his own as the leading rep-
tile of the tropics. He constricts or chokes his prey. He
can swallow an ordinary dog or young goat. The average
size of one of them is from five to ten inches in diameter
and from twelve to twenty feet long.

There are other snakes, such as the long python, the black or egg-eater, and the casava snake. The last is the most dreaded of the reptiles in the country. Its bite is considered fatal by the natives.

The python is the longest snake in the world. It is of ordinary size, from one inch to inch and a half in diameter and from twenty to fifty feet long.

The double-headed snake is the greatest mystery of the globe. I have seen a commission from the Smithsonian Institute, in Washington, hunting the two-headed snakes in Liberia. They had not found any of them the last I knew. I have seen them and often stopped to play with them. They look like a big fish-worm, only they are black. I very much delighted in teasing them, because when you touch one end he runs back the other way as fast as he did forward. He is something like two feet long. There are several kinds of lizards. The largest of the species is called "gv.ana." It looks like a young alligator, only it is spotted.

Insects

The mosquito heads the list here, and the malarial mosquito is prevalent in Liberia. If the tall grass is kept down around the dwelling-house and good screens in the windows and doors, with mosquito nets over and around the bed, there is not much to fear from malaria. It is safe, however, to take two and one-half grains of quinine every day.

The tsetse fly is said by scientists to produce sleeping disease. It is not so plentiful in Liberia as in other portions of Africa. But it will make you know it is there if you ride up and down the rivers upon the canoes. It is just a little larger than an ordinary house fly and carries its probocis straight before it.

Ants are the dread of the country. At the head of that army is the "high strung" driver ant. He is three times as large as any ant in the United States. He travels from place to place in long lines or caravans. The line is often one-fourth of a mile long. The big general ants stand upon hind legs on the outside of the line and whip the slave ants that are made to carry the loads. They especially like palm oil and hog meat. They travel long distances to obtain such things. The only objection we have to them is that they never send notice of their intended arrival. Their favorite time to attack is in the night. They drive all other insects, and even all classes of animals, the elephant not excepted, before them. The soldiers are aroused from their cots and the sentinel must beat a hasty retreat from the army of invaders. You need not get up. Have a lime near your bed. Sprinkle a little of the juice around your bed and finish your much-wanted nap.

The crooked-tail scorpion is dangerous. The bite is hard to cure. The centipede likes to get under the pillow. I cannot say that he means any harm, but he just likes a nice warm place to domicile. There are more thousand-legs in Africa than in any other portion of the world. I am glad that they decide to stay out of doors in their place. There are no house flies. The ''mission ants'' make up for them. Their bite is severe and poisonous.

CHAPTER VII

Setting up a Stable Government in Liberia

Emigrants to Liberia

The following table shows the progress of emigration to Liberia and the number of boats used for same from the year 1820 to 1852:

Year	Boats	People	Year	Boats	People
1820	1	88	1837	3	138
1821	1	33	1838	2	109
1822	1	37	1839	2	47
1823	2	65	1840	2	115
1824	1	103	1841	3	85
1825	1	66	1842	2	248
1826	2	182	1843	2	85
1827	3	129	1844	3	170
1828	1	165	1845	1	187
1829	2	203	1846	3	89
1830	3	235	1847	2	51
1831	4	421	1848	5	441
1832	7	796	1849	5	422
1833	5	270	1850	6	504
1834	1	127	1851	5	676
1835	4	146	1852	7	630
1836	4	234			

The agitation of the Civil War caused decrease of emigrants.

Colonial Agents and Governors

Following is a list of Colonial Agents and Governors from the founding of the country to Independence:

1820-1 —Bacon, Bankson, Crozier.

1821-2 —Eli Ayers, Frederick James.

1822-5 —Jehudi Ashman.

1825-6 —Elijah Johnson.

1827 —Jihudi Ashman.

1828 —Lott Carey.

1828 —Richard Randall (after death of Lott Carey).

1829-34—William Mecklin.

1834   —John B. Pinney.

1835   —Ezekiel Shinner.

1836   —A. D. Williams.

1839   —Thomas Buchanan, Governor Colonial Gov'ment.

1841   —Joseph J. Roberts, Lieutenant-Governor.

1847   —J. J. Roberts, Governor.

Increase of Inhabitants and Territory.

The State of Mississippi sent out a Colony to Sinoe. The State of Pennsylvania sent another Colony from the Young Men's Association.

At this time it began to dawn upon the leaders of affairs that there was immediate need of a stable form of Government. Each settlement making and trying to enforce its own laws, very often caused conflicts that were far from agreeable. Therefore, they fully decided that all the country should be united under one code of laws. Accordingly, a committee was appointed to draft laws for the Government and for the advice of its citizens. The Committee appointed by the Colonization Society for this purpose consisted of Charles F. Mercer, Samuel L. Southard, Matthew Saint Clair Clark, and Elisha Wittlesey.

The first provision brought a spirited discussion. This gave Missionaries and Traders a right to own real estate in Liberia. It was finally voted down, however, and it was fully decided that no white man should have the right to own land in Liberia.

Boundary Disputes—Loss of Kanre Lahun

More recently events have occurred in the Northwestern corner of Liberia, the native town and district of Kanre Lahun, which have brought Liberia into an irritating controversy. Briefly stated, the town was in occupation of a British command when the Delimitation Commission of 1903 discovered that it was located in Liberian territory.

In 1904, a native war broke out in this district, and it

was alleged that raids were made into British territory. Through the British Consul-General at Monrovia, permission was granted by the authorities at Monrovia to British soldiers to enter this district for the purpose of quelling the disturbance. When once in the territory, they refused to evacuate.

About this time, France also demanded that Liberia fully control her stations upon the boundary to prevent disturbance between French and Liberian subjects. Then added the postscript that if Liberia failed to secure the safety of French subjects, France would have to take charge of the stations.

France and England have sat one on the one side and the other upon the other side like massive bull dogs, watching each other across Liberia. As England had taken Liberian territory in the North, France felt compelled to take some from the South. So, upon some petty pretext, she took her troops and deliberately marched down to the Cavalla River, into Liberia.

In 1924, France again encroached upon the rights of Liberia by marching over the boundary line into Liberia on the East. This caused an uproar in Liberia. I have never seen the feeling so tense. During a holiday reception at the Mansion, President King spoke concerning the trouble with France as follows: ''Say no word or do no act that may be interpreted ill will or violence to the French representative or to the French Republic. Give the Government time and she will settle all matters amicably in a diplomatic way.''

The citizens of Liberia were desirous of settling it another way. But they are orderly and law-abiding people; therefore they adhered to the enunciations of the Government. Hon. Edwin Barclay, Secretary of State, was hurried to America, and the French withdrew.

Most Important Laws

The most important laws are given below:

Article 1. The legislative powers herein granted shall be vested in a Governor and Council of Liberia, but all laws enacted by them shall be subject to revocation by the Colonization Society.

Article 2. The Council shall consist of members elected by the people from the different settlements, and shall be apportioned among them according to a just ratio of representation.

The Commonwealth shall be devided into two Counties. Monrovia, Caldwell and New Georgia shall constitute one County and shall be entitled to send six representatives. The County shall be named Mesurado. Bassa Cove, Marshall, Bexley and Edina shall constitute one County, and shall send four representatives.

Article 15. The judicial power of the Commonwealth of Liberia shall be vested in one Supreme Court and in such inferior Courts as the Governor and Council may from time to time ordain and establish.

Article 20. There shall be no slavery in the Commonwealth.

Article 21. There shall be no dealing in slaves by any citizen of the Commonwealth, either within or without the bounds of the same.

Article 23. The right of trial by jury and petition shall be inviolate.

Article 25. Every male citizen of the age of twenty-one shall have the right of suffrage.

Article 26. All elections shall be by ballot.

The new Constitution and the new Governor (Buchanan) came out upon the Saluda and arrived at Monrovia April 1, 1839. After the Governor had been received in full military style he assembled the citizens to hear the new laws.

They liked them with one exception, that being the veto power of the Governor. This was soon explained and adjusted, and all the citizens of Monrovia took the oath of allegiance. Their example was soon followed by the other settlements. "It is wise and good," they said, "and a good stepping-stone to independent sovereignty."

The first session of the Legislature was held in Monrovia in September, 1839. During this session a post-office was established; also a school and asylum begun.

Public Schools Established

Be it enacted by the Governor and Council of the Commonwealth in Legislature assembled, That there shall be established in each settlement and township that is or may hereafter be established or formed in this Commonwealth, one common school, same to be under supervision or control of a school committee to be created for that purpose by the Governor and Council.

"The Golden Age of Liberia"

At this time, Liberia had grown to possess five hundred thousand acres of rich land, where the finest vegetables and fruits in the world could be grown. It had four printing presses and two newspapers—"African Luminar" and "Liberian Herald." It had twenty-one Churches and thirty Ministers of the Gospel. They held monthly prayer service in which Baptists, Methodists and Presbyterians joined.

They had a school at Monrovia, two lyceums, and Temperance Society. Her traders and merchants were busy upon the rivers and upon the coast. The Liberians owned six vessels of ninety tons' capacity that plied up and down the coast. They grew large crops of sugar cane, and besides supplying the Colonists, shipped sugar abroad. Lott Carey, in his day, shipped 6,000 pounds of coffee to Richmond, Va.

At this time, the Liberians were seriously in need of a

steamship of their own. And the Maryland Colonization Society was willing to co-operate with them in that scheme. A joint stock company was proposed to be entered into by the Liberians on the one side and the American Negroes on the other. The ship was to be manned by Colored seamen. The Maryland Legislature granted them a charter, and stockholders were asked to come forward and take shares. The Liberians subscribed liberally, but the Americans failed. The white people, however, came to their rescue. Notable among those who helped was Dr. Hall.

The steamer was launched and called the "Liberian Packet." It made several successful trips, carrying out freight and passengers.

Many of the native tribes came forward, and of their own volition desired to join the Liberians—" 'Mericans,'' as they styled them. They had found that the Liberians being among them protected them from the raids of the slavers as well as from the treachery and covetousness of their own tribesmen.

King Bromley, four miles below Millsburg, on the St. Paul River, accepted terms of peace and signed the document drawn up by the Governor. The Cru people, down the coast, while they would not sell any of their land to the Liberians, signed terms of peace and agreed not to dispose of their land to any other power.

It was about this time, after organizing the Colonial Government and preparing to celebrate their victory of the 1st of December, Hilary Teag, the poet of Liberia, sang forth:

> Land of the mighty dead:
> Here science once displayed,
>   And art their charms;
> Here awful Pharaoh swayed
> Great nations who obeyed;
> Here distant monarch laid
>   Their vanquished charms.

They hold us in survey,
They loud proclaim;
From Pyrimidal Hall,
From Carnac's sculptured wall,
From Thebes they loudly call:
"Retake your fame"!

All hail Liberia, hail!
Arise and now prevail
O'er all thy foes
In truth and righteousness,
In all the arts of peace
Advance and still increase,
Though hosts oppose.

At the loud call we rise
And press towards the prize
In glory's race.
All redolent of fame,
The land to which we came
We'll breathe inspiring praise
In Jesus' name.

Here liberty shall dwell,
Here justice shall prevail
Over all this sphere.
To this fair virtue's dome,
Meek Innocence may come
And find a peaceful home
And know no fear.

Storm After the Calm

The devil never allows the human race to sit down in ease too long in any country. One man by the name of Lange, an American white man, went down the coast in the neighborhood of Bassa-Cove and erected a Baracoon and began to buy slaves. Governor Buchanan sent him word to leave Liberia, but he paid no heed to the warning. Again he sent to inform him that if he failed to leave at once he would have to use severe means to expel him. At this he laughed and fortified his stronghold. Governor Buchanan called the citizens together with the Council and explained the matters to them. It was fully decided to take arms against them. Who would go? Thirty men volunteered at once. Many joined them from the settlement of New Georgia. The infantry was sent over land and the arms and ammunition for supplies were started upon the sea. But on account of contrary winds, the next day, to the surprise and chagrin of the Governor, the sloop returned.

Just then an English cruiser brought into harbor a slaver and delivered it and its cargo to the Colonists.

Upon this transport, Governor Buchanan and his men went forth. On reaching the field of conflict, it became a puzzle as to how they could get information from the shore as to how the battle was progressing. A native canoe, approaching them, informed the Governor that the " 'Mericans be in the Baracoon." The Governor feared that the slaver would be thought for Lange and his cohorts. How to get them information to the contrary puzzled him. At length an American sailor decided to take the risk. He went ashore and was nearly murdered by the natives that rushed on him, but Elijah Johnson, discovering that the messenger was on his side, just got up in time to shoot down the native that had drawn his knife to stab the messenger.

Governor Buchanan and his men now ventured ashore under the protecting fire from their guns aboard the schooner. The Baracoon was soon destroyed and the town laid in ashes. Lange absconded to regions unknown in the night.

A message was dispatched to the chiefs to come at once and bring all of their slaves. Next morning Bah Gray appeared upon the beach with a white flag. But he was shaking with fear, and it took much persuasion to entice him to appear before the Governor, although he was surrounded with 300 warriors. He finally came and surrendered and delivered over all of his slaves. He claimed to be sorry for the part which he took against the " 'Mericans." The Euphrates, with the Liberians, returned in triumph to Monrovia. Several of the soldiers had been wounded, among them was Captain Elijah Johnson; none, however, was seriously hurt. It was reported that the natives had ten killed and many wounded.

Gatoomba

They were not long to rejoice over their victory down the coast, for trouble was brewing upon their very threshold. One King named Gatoomba, living in the rear of Millsburg (so named for Mills and Burgess), angered at the Colonists because they prevented him from trading in slaves, was determined to make havoc of the "new-comers." The Liberians had several warnings concerning the intentions of their enemies, and the people of Heddington began to bestir themselves.

They did not move too soon, for Gatoomba and his crowd were upon them. They ran in and surprised them and gave them a bloody battle. But one man, Harris, with the strong assistance of the other settlers, stubbornly resisted their assault and finally drove them back into the jungles.

Although Gatoomba was defeated and for the time being seemed checked, yet Governor Buchanan desired to follow him to his den and make an end of him and his followers. There was, moreover, fear that the interior tribes might join him and make such a united attack that the Liberians would be entirely blotted out. Accordingly, Governor Buchanan organized an army of 300 soldiers, under General Roberts, and taking one field-piece, set out sixty miles away into the interior to Gatoomba's stronghold.

The very first day they became almost exhausted by having to pull the old cannon over bridges and through swamps, and therefore they decided the second day to leave it concealed in the forest. As they marched onward, they saw nothing of the enemy until the second day. Resting in an abandoned town the night before, they arose early the next morning and proceeded towards Gatoomba's town, not far distant. They had not journeyed far before they found the enemy alert and raining bullets upon them from behind trees and rocks. But they had no time for skirmishes; onward they must go.

Upon emerging from a swamp, almost overcome with fatigue, suddenly they found themselves before Gatoomba's fortifications. And notwithstanding the soldiers were almost exhausted from the journey over the long, rugged road, they drove home the shot and swivel through every conveivable crevice in the walls. It was soon seen that American fire was too hot for the native men and they speedily retreated. The Liberians were surprised that the victory was so soon won. General Roberts, however, as a war measure, marched into the fortifications, placed the Liberian standard upon the walls, and proclaimed the battle fought and won. The soldiers refreshed themselves and rested that night, and the next day burned the town and departed. Gatoomba had his brother's bones covered up in the house as a "gree gree," but it did not work that time.

When Governor Buchanan returned to Monrovia, he was very much surprised to find many of the Kings from the interior coming down to Monrovia to join the Government. They had been watching the line of battle and were impressed with the dignity of the Liberians, and sought, therefore, to join them. They were cordially accepted and received into the body politic.

Now, Governor Buchanan's labors were almost over. He took one other trip to Bassa-Cove to settle some matters needing his assistance, he contracted a fever, which caused his death. He was buried with honors at Bassa-Cove.

It will be of interest to my readers to hear a part of the oration delivered upon that occasion by Rev. Hilary Teag:

"Not infrequently to be met with in the history of nations is the fact that some individual's name, from a concurrence of circumstances, carry terror wherever it is heard among his or his country's foes. The brilliant and continuous chain of circumstances which crowned the campaigns of Napoleon is to be accounted for as much from this fact as from his universally admitted skill in their science and courage on the battlefield of combat. Victory was supposed to hover over his march and in the field and to perch upon their sword. Thus, their enemies, palsied with terror, were prepared at the onset to yield an easy victory or seek safety in an ignominious flight or an unconditional surrender.

"For similar coincidences, united with the strict integrity and good faith which marked all Governor Buchanan's intercourse with the natives (readily conceding to them all their rights, and inflexibly demanding his), the like impressions pervaded their minds. The bare encounter with him in the hall of palaver or in the field of fight was regarded by them as an earnest of defeat. Never was a man more feared and respected by the natives than Governor Buchanan, nor is there a man in all the Colonies the influence of whose presence can so perfectly check or hold in abeyance their blustering passions as did the presence of our lamented Governor. Frank and open, he was a stranger to duplicity. He possessed largely the charity which thinketh no evil and acknowledges readily whatever was commendable in the character of his enemies. He presented a harmonious unity of dignity and gentleness. To sum up his character, he was a Christian and a gentleman."

The duties of his office now fell upon Lieutenant Governor J. J. Roberts. And as so many of my readers do not know

that the Liberians do things up to date, I now quote from
the official records the manner in which he was inducted
into office.

"Agency House, Bassa-Cove,
September 3, 1841.
"To General J. J. Roberts,
Monrovia.

"Sir,—The sudden and mournful dispensation by
which we have been bereaved of our late Chief Magistrate
places you in such a position to us and the Commonwealth
of Liberia as to compel us to throw all our weight of public
care upon you. As under the guidance and teaching of your
illustrious predecessor, we have had inculcated in us lessons of economy and principles of Republican liberty, permit us to hope that being favored with the blessings of
heaven, you will be governed by the same imperishable principles and to the same end. How deeply we condole with
you in the almost irreparable loss we have sustained need
not here be stated; but be assured of our co-operation in
every emergency, of our prayers for the success of all our
undertakings, and that our public affliction may be sancti-
fied to our public good.

(Signed)   "Wm. Weaver.
Nathaniel Harris.
John Day.
Lewis Sheridan."

Not many of our educated Colored people of America can
draw up a better paper.

Governor Roberts entered with solemnity upon the rugged task. He was also appointed by the American Colonization Society of America, being the first Colored man des-
ignated by them for that position.

The Colonists experienced great disturbances upon the
coast on account of the slave-traders on the one hand and
the English traders on the other. The slavers persisted in

Hon. J. J. Roberts, First President of Liberia

their mission of degradation, while the traders revolted against the rightful authority of Liberia to the soil. They refused to pay customs duties, and many broils were engaged in by the authorities and the traders. The Colonization Society was also growing reluctant to assist the Colony. And it was generally conceded that they were coming to a full-grown manhood and could now attend to their own affairs.

Independence Declared

The Colonists were thinking likewise. Therefore, finding no other way out of the dilemma, a Constitutional Convention was called in Monrovia in July, 1847, to draw up a Constitution and declare the Independence of the Country.

Governor Roberts proclaimed a day of thanksgiving and prayer on behalf of the Convention assembled. That was three weeks of toil and study, but finally they were ready to submit their findings to the people.

When they had completed their work, they felt like a bird that had escaped the snare of the fowler. They often exclaimed, "Our help is in God who made the heavens and the earth." Hear their announcement to the world.

"We, the representatives of the people of the Commonwealth of Liberia, in Convention assembled, invested with authority to form a new Government, relying upon the aid and protection of the Great Arbiter of human events, do hereby, in the name and on behalf of the people of this Commonwealth, publish and declare the said Commonwealth a free, sovereign and independent State, the name and title of the Republic of Liberia.

"We, the people of the Republic of Liberia, were originally the inhabitants of the United States of America. In some parts of that country, we were debarred by law from all the rights and privileges of men; in other parts, public sentiment more powerful than law frowned us down. We were everywhere shut out from all civil offices.

"We were excluded from all participation in the Government. We were taxed without our consent. We were compelled to contribute to the resources of a country which gave us no protection We were made a separate and distinct class, and against us every avenue of improvement was effectually closed. Strangers from all lands of a color different from ours were preferred before us. We uttered our complaints but they were unattended to or only met by alleging the peculiar institutions of the country. All hope of a favorable change in our country was thus wholly extinguished in our bosom and we looked abroad for some asylum from the deep degradation.

"The West Coast of Africa was the place selected by American benevolence and philanthropy for our future home. Moved beyond influences that depress us, it was hoped that we would be allowed to enjoy those rights and privileges and exercise and improve those faculties which the God of nature has given to us in common with all mankind.

"Liberia, already the happy home of thousands who were doomed victims of oppression, and thus far our highest hopes have been relaized. Our courts of justice are open equally to the stranger and the citizen for the redress of grievances, for the remedy of injuries and for the punishment of crime.

"Our numerous and well-attended schools attest our efforts and our desire for improvement of our children. Our Churches for the worship of our Creator, every where to be seen, bear testimony to our piety and to our acknowledgment of His providence.

"The native African, bowing down with us before the altar of the living God, declares that from us, feeble as we

are, the light of Christianity has gone forth; while upon
that curse of curses—the slave-trader—has fallen a deadly
blight. as far as our influence extends.   Therefore, in the
name of humanity, virtue and religion; in the name of the
great God, our common Creator and our common Judge, we
appeal to the Nations of Christendom and earnestly and respectfully ask them that they will regard us with sympathy
and friendly consideration to which the character of our
condition entitles us, and to extend unto us that comity
which marks the friendly intercourse of civilized and independent communities.''

Signed: S. Benedict, J. N. Lewis, H. Teage, Bev-
erly R Wilson, Elijah Johnson, J. B. Grippon, Mesurado
County; John Day, A. W. Gardner, Amos Herring, Eph-
riam Titler, Grand Bassa County; R. E. Murray, Sinoe
County.

The Flag of the Republic was afterwards adopted, as well
as the Seal of the Republic.

Its Flag consisted of six red stripes alternating with five
white ones, displayed longitudinally.   In the upper angle
of the Flag, near the spear, is a square blueground covering in depth five stripes, in the center of which is a white
star.

The imprint of the Seal is a dove on the wing with a letter in its mouth, a view of the ocean with the sun rising, a
sailing ship in sght.   Upon the beach, a palm tree, at the
foot of which is a shovel and a plow.   Across the Seal are
the words, ''The love of Liberty brought us here.''

It is needless to tell you that on the 26th of July, 1847,
when the declaration was declared, was a great day in Monrovia and in the history of the Republic!

People gathered from every where, and a lively program
was executed.   The Government's health was drunk in the
purest water of Mesurado's gurgling springs.   Prophets,

optimistic of the glorious dawn, burst forth with visions of
rapture. Rev. J. S. Payne was chosen to deliver the oration, but upon the occasion of raising the Flag of the Republic, our illustrious poet could not hold his peace; therefore, I am pleased to give you the last and greatest poem of
Hon. Hilary Teage. He has now been elected the first Secretary of State. As the guns from the fort thundered forth
their twenty-one notes in salute, Hilary, in the Mansion,
sang out—

> Wake, every tuneful string,
> To God loud praises bring;
>   Wake, heart and tongue,
> In strains of melody
> And choral harmony,
> Sing, for the oppressed are free:
>   Wake, cheerful song!
>
> See Mesurado's height
> Illumin'd with new-born light.
>   Lo, the one Star!
> Now it ascends the skies;
> Lo, the deep darkness flies,
> While new-born glories rise
>   And shine afar.
>
> Shout the loud jubilee,
> Afric once more is free!
>   Break forth with joy,
> Let Nillus' fettered tongue,
> Let Niger join the song,
> And Congo loud and long
>   Glad strains employ.
>
> Star in the East, shine forth,
> Proclaim a nation's birth:
>   Ye nations hear.
> This is our natal day,
> And we our homage pay
> To the O Lord we pray,
>   Lord, hear our prayer.

Shine, life-creating ray,
Proclaim approaching day,
Throw wide thy blaze.
Lo! savage Hottentot,
Bosjeman from his cot,
And nations long forgot,
Astonished gaze!
All hail Liberia, hail!
Favored of God, all hail!
Hail, happy land.
From virtue ne'er remove,
By peace and truth and love,
And wisdom from above,
So shalt thou stand.

Montgomery, from across the mighty deep, caught the strains of freedom and sang:

Muse, take the harp of prophecy, behold!
The glories of a brighter age unfold.
Friends of the outcast, view the accomplished plan:
The Negro towering to the height of man.

I know that you are anxious to turn the page from this pure Negro joy, but you must hear Liberia's national anthem first. It is said to be the most beautiful national anthem in the world. The words of the anthem were composed by Liberians, the Hon. Mr. Tuning being one of the leading figures. The music was set to it by Mr. Luka, who had just come from America. He was also a Colored man, so that the entire anthem was composed and set to music by Colored Liberians.

All hail Liberia, hail! All hail Liberia, hail!
This glorious land of liberty shall long be ours;
Though new her name, great be her fame and mighty be
       her powers.
In joy and gladness, with our hearts united,
We'll shout the freedom of a race benighted:
Long live Liberia, happy land!
A home of glorious liberty by God's command.

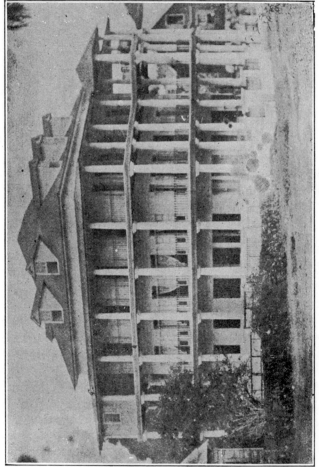

White House, Liberia

All hail Liberia, hail! All hail Liberia, hail!
In union, strong success is sure, we cannot fail;
With God above, our rights to prove, we will o'er all prevail.
With heart and hand, our country's cause defending,
We'll meet the foe with valor unpretending—
Long live Liberia, happy land!
A home of glorious liberty by God's command.

The new Constitution was accepted by the people on the 27th of September, 1847, and on the 5th of October a regular election took place. Hon. J. J. Roberts was elected First President, and Nathaniel Brander was chosen Vice-President. The President was elected for only two years.

The President delivered his message to the First National Legislature in January, 1848, at which time he also took the oath of office. Shortly after adjournment of the Legislature, President Roberts, accompanied by two Commissioners, visited the United States. The Commissioners were Rev. James S. Payne and Nathaniel Brander. Making a safe and successful passage, they arrived in Boston in May, 1848. They were kindly received by the American Colonization Society and were enabled to speedily adjust matters pertaining to the Liberian Government.

The Colonization Society ceded to Liberia all lands except that needed for settlement of the recaptured Africans and for Missionary use.

President Roberts Visits Home

President Roberts visited his friends in Norfolk, Va., and was everywhere received according to his station.

He left America and visited France and England. France readily acknowledged the Independence of Liberia; England soon followed. Having finished their work, with much delight they turned their faces homeward. They were soon back beneath the Lone Star and received with great joy by the people.

Beginning of the Baptist Church among the Cru People

CHAPTER VIII

MISSIONS AND SCHOOLS

Since we have traced the Republic of Liberia from its
incipiency as a mere handful of stranded human beings
upon "Perseverance Island," in 1822, to this glorious period, 1850, let us now look around and see what is being done
spiritually and educationally. A beautiful poem by William P. Tappan is appropriate here.

While on the distant Hindoo shore
  Messiah's cross is reared;
While pagan votaries bow no more
  With idol blood besmeared;

While palestine again doth hear
  The Gospel's joyful sound;
While Islam's crescents disappear
  From Calvary's holy ground:

Shall not Afric's fated land
  With news of grace be blest?
Shall not Ethiopia's band
  Enjoy the promised rest?

Ye heralds of a Saviour's love,
  To Afric's regions fly;
O haste, and let compassion move
  For millions doomed to die!

Blest Jesus, who for those hast bled,
  Wilt Thou the captives free?
And Ethiopia, too, shall spread
  Her ransomed hands to Thee.

Lott Carey the First Missionary

He was sent out under the auspices of the General Convention of Virginia, the Missionary Society of the First
Baptist Church, and under the watchful care of the Colonization Society. The writer will not dwell at length upon

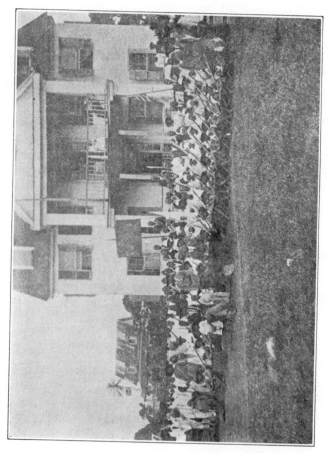

National Baptist Mission at Bassa, Liberia

his career here, as one entire chapter has been given to his history and labors. Lott Carey, during the short time he lived in Liberia (six years), established Mission Schools in Monrovia, Caldwell, Millsburg, Cape Mount and Careysburg

As incredible as it may seem, the Baptists, for one hundred years afterward, have not gone one step further than did Lott Carey in six short years. (African Repository, Vols. 1-7.)

The Lutheran Mission was Next

The Lutheran Mission began in Liberia in 1825 and has moved steadily onward since that time. They have eight stations, well manned, running from Monrovia back to the boundary. They are the only Mission I know in Liberia that has a chain of stations running clear across the country.

Their Trade School has produced some fine artists for the Republic. You are not able to find a village in the whole of Mesurado County in which you will not find a shoemaker, tailor, or some tradesman from Muhlenburg Mission. The Mission has been a great blessing to Liberia.

They have a fine Hospital at Muhlenburg, and paid Dr. Fusek $6,000 salary, as Mission Doctor, per year. Statistics for 1925-6: Stations, 8; Missionaries, 30; students enrolled, 710.

Northern and Southern Baptists

About this period, the Northern and Southern Baptists entered Liberia. The Northern Society worked mostly through Liberians. They are said to have had at one time 200 Missionaries. The Liberians of that time speak of them maintaining a Church and School in almost every settlement. They withdrew and went to the Congo Country.

The Southern Baptists did a very good work in Liberia. Their earnest Missionary, Rev. John Day, is affectionately remembered in Liberia until today. He established a large

Sueh Industrial Mission, Established by Miss E. B. Delaney, with Arthington School, N. B. C.

Mission in Monrovia, known as "Day's Mission." The foundations of the brick structure are still visible upon Crown Hill, Monrovia, beside the home of Mr. Lincoln Vincent. Mr. Day reported, for a single year of his school, 350 pupils. Many of the men around Monrovia, according to A. B. Stubblefield, Sr., got their start at his Mission School. During his encumbency in the City of Monrovia, he was also Pastor of Providence Baptist Church. It was during his time that the Southern Baptist Convention gave assistance to Providence Baptist Church, and it was remodeled in its present state. They withdrew from Liberia and went to Nigeria, English district.

Revs. Colley, Bouey, Coles and McKinney labored for many years under very trying circumstances at Bendu, Cape Mount.

The next Baptist man to follow Lott Carey was Mr. Capps, a graduate of Shaw University. He settled at Brewerville, and would have done a noble work had it not been that he fell an early victim to the malarial fever. Hattie Pressley, a beautiful character, also gave up her life at Cape Mount for the redemption of Africa.

All of our Missionaries of the Baptist Church deserve mention, for they have all fought bravely against malaria, leopards and death. Rev. J. O. Hayes, in Liberia about fifty years; Rev. W. H. Thomas, A. B., Mrs. Cora Thomas, Rev. and Mrs. Burke, Rev. and Mrs. E. D. Hubbard, Rev. and Mrs. Douglass, Rev. and Mrs. D. R. Horton, Misses Minnie Lyons, Mattie Banks, and Clarise Gooding, Mrs. F. B. Watson, Misses Delaney, Morris, and Williamson; later came Rev. and Mrs. Bouey. They are under Dr. East.

Rev. W. H. Thomas has done, with the assistance of Mrs. Thomas, a splendid work in Liberia. With the help of the writer and the other Lott Carey Missionaries, he has been enabled to erect a fine cement building at Brewerville, just fifteen miles from Monrovia. It is located in a civilized settlement, but the native people in the surrounding district bring their children to the School to be taught English especially, and any other thing that will make them like the white men.

Our Work at Monrovia

Dr. Alexander, just before his departure for the better land, sent out a message to the field that some of us should spread out from Brewerville. That was indeed providential, for the practice of medicine at Brewerville was fast getting the better of me, having to go out so often at night through rough roads and swamps without bridges.

Minister James L. Curtis was sent out to Monrovia as American Minister and Consul-General about this time. Mr. R. C. Bundy, who was the Secretary, had remained in the Country a long time, and was due to take a furlough to America, providing any suitable American citizen could be found to take his place. Hon. James L. Curtis was a very polished lawyer, from New York, and was courteous and congenial. I often thought, after visiting him, that he was very nice. At last, one day he explained to me that he wanted to borrow me from my Mission for three months until he could get out another clerk for the Legation, as the one he had was leaving.

I explained the matter to the Missionaries at Brewerville, and they gave their consent. Therefore, I took up my abode at the big city of the Republic. Now, "big city" out there does not mean that you are at all isolated from heathenism, for wretched, uncivilized, poor, half-nude, dejected Aborigines wander through the streets of Monrovia, "unwept, unhonored and unsung." I was in the Legation eleven months and twenty-one days. Dr. Alexander, the Corresponding Secretary of the Lott Carey Foreign Mission Society, also consented to my serving in that capacity.

C. C. BOONE, JR., AND RACHEL H. C. BOONE
They were Born in the Republic of Liberia

The work was arduous. I had to fill the place of clerk and secretary. The Liberians prophesied that I would have many assistants to keep up that work. Minister Lyon had five clerks, but I was never helped one hour. During this year that I was in the Legation, I was compelled to give up the practice of medicine and my Mission work. I also gave up my salary from the Mission Society. The Government promised $80 per month, and paid it.

Back in the Mission

As soon as Mr. Bundy came back to take his job, I returned to my work. Should say, however, that the Minister offered me blanks to send in my application to become permanent clerk of the Legation, and I refused to fill them because Almighty God was before him and had given me a life-long commission as ambassador of eternal glory to the unsaved.

School in Monrovia

At once I opened a day School in Monrovia. The College of West Africa could not accommodate all the children of Monrovia, and the poor Baptist children had no School.

Finding Lott Carey's Grave

One day I was talking with Rev. W. H. Johnson, of Liberia, and he said to me, "You know that Lott Carey was buried up yonder in the cemetery?" I said, "No; it is not possible." I begged him to come and go up there and find it. When it grew cooler, we did go and walked all over the place. The cemetery was then grown over with tall grass. We could not find it. The second time we looked for it, but could not find it. The third time we looked for it, but could not find it. He was the only man who had the least knowledge as to the location of the grave. Finally, he said to me, "Let us wait until the grass is burned off, and then we can see better and can find the grave." So we just had to wait until the grass was burned.

After the grass fire, Rev. Johnson came to Monrovia again, and I said to him, "Come, let us find that grave." He consented to help me look for it. We went out there, and soon he called me and I ran where he was. He said, "Boone, here is the footstone; the headstone has fallen down, but I am sure this is the footstone." I took a short stick and scratched in the sand and found the tombstone buried in the sand. I thanked him just as much as I could.

The next morning I was up by time. I went out and hired three boys. I went in the loft and pulled out a tent that I had used more than five hundred miles back in Congo for evangelistic work, and carried it up to the cemetery and put it down under the shade of a big plum tree. I carried my cook pots and food and water. I also bought a barrel of cement and rolled it up there. I bought some pine boards and had them carried up. Then I took the trowel that I had used to fix up my wife's grave in Congo and carried it up there.

When I found that the tombstone was buried so deeply in the sand (it had been down there twenty-five years), I sent and got some weeding hoes and dug it out of the ground. I made the boys bring as many stones as they could find, and made up the grave. I also built up the base for the stone. I learned the brick mason's trade by building brick Churches in Africa. When the stone was erected (I mean when it was washed off and erected), then I cemented over the grave. That was a happy day's work. I took down the tent and went back to my home in the city.

Next day I secured the services of Mr. Humphrey Taylor, a very good photographer, and had a picture made while I stood by Lott Carey's Tomb.

I could not stop here. I went to Providence Baptist Church and got their consent to use their Church building for the decoration day of Lott Carey's grave. The day

Rev. C. C. Boone, M. D., at the Grave of Lott Carey.

came, and a large crowd marched down to the cemetery. I explained how I had found the grave. Rev. Thomas read the inscriptions upon the tombstone. We deposited our flowers and departed. I had prepared a large cross that was carried by two school boys. This attracted much attention. Many of the citizens went with us. *155798*

The People in America Rejoiced

The greatest possible enthusiasm was manifested by the people of the United States, and especially the constituents of the Lott Carey Mission Society. Sister Sallie Mial, of North Carolina, wrote to ask me how much expense I had been put to in finding and fixing up the grave of Lott Carey. I sent her back an itemized account amounting, I think, to some $44, and she sent me a check from the "What I Can Society" of North Carolina children, for $100 (one hundred dollars).

Providence Baptist Church

The Church, as I have already stated, was organized in the City of Richmond, Va., and as soon as the Colonists landed in Monrovia they began at once to gather and hold service. At first, all of the Colonists worshiped together. Several attempts were made to begin the Methodist Episcopal Church, but its real beginning in Liberia was in 1833, upon the arrival of Melvin B. Cox, their first Missionary.

When I went to live in Monrovia, I attended the Baptist Church. I found the members struggling to keep their services interesting. The great need of the Liberian Baptists is an efficient ministry. The Church at Monrovia was suffering from the same need.

In 1918, by unanimous vote, the writer was called to take charge of the Providence Baptist Church and was promised a salary of $250 per year.

Celebration of Easter

The Church edifice was badly in need of repairs, so when I took charge they asked me for plans with which to increase the finance of the Church. I at once recommended the celebration of Easter and a grand rally in that connection. This was the first Baptist Church in the whole Republic to observe Easter. We had an interesting program by the Sunday School. I preached the first Easter sermon in a Baptist Church in Liberia. We raised on that occasion the very magnificent sum of *five hundred dollars in cash*. Needless to tell you, the Church soon took on new life and its rightful place as the First Church of the Republic.

The One Hundredth Anniversary

The Church was founded there at the same time as the Government, in 1822, so in 1922 it was one hundred years old. Great preparation was made for that celebration. The Church had granted me a furlough to go to America, and I had the great pleasure of bringing out the second Hartshorn College girl as my companion—Miss Rachel Tharps, of Richmond, Va. My first wife, Miss Eva Roberta Coles, of Charlottesville, Va., had demised in the Congo.

The Church building was thoroughly ventilated and repaired, both inside and out, and was very presentable for the great occasion. The Government of Liberia also celebrated the landing of the Pilgrims, but the celebration held by the Church was first on December 17, 1922. I give here some excerpts from the program rendered upon that occasion.

Address of Welcome

The "Address of Welcome" was delivered by Col. Jos. S. Dennis, District Commissioner, who said, in part:

"The task of welcoming to this Commonwealth the exercises of the celebration of the One Hundredth Anniversary

PROVIDENCE CHURCH BUILDING
Church Organized by Lott Carey in 1822

of the founding of the Baptist denomination in the Republic of Liberia has, on account of my official position, been assigned to me. In consequence of which, I now appear before you.

"This is as it should be, for the whole of Liberia has been greatly benefitted by the little movement started by the immortal Lott Carey one hundred years ago on the good ship 'Elizabeth,' sailing to these shores from the United States, bearing her precious cargo of men and women, pioneers of what has turned out to be the great Republic of Liberia.

"I say, great Republic of Liberia, for Liberia is great. Great in achievements and great in possibilities. The very fact that we, the sons and daughters of those pioneer fathers and mothers, are today celebrating the one hundredth anniversary of the founding of the Baptist denomination in Liberia, which can boast of an unbroken record of continuous service, extending her borders from Cape Mount Territory, on the north, to Maryland County on the south, with numerous Church-houses and school-houses and a numerical strength comprising over 4,000 adherents, is in itself a great achievement. And when we note the fact that the Baptists of Liberia have for many decades of this century of existence been deprived of foreign support and had to exist as best they could by their own local efforts, this shows that not only the past is great with achievements, but the future is great with possibilities. Without any hesitation whatsoever, the other branches of the Christian Church in Liberia look up to the Baptist as the mother Church.

"Ladies and gentlemen, we are standing today on holy ground. On this spot, where the Providence Baptist Church now stands erected to God and dedicated to His worship, once stood the site of demon worship. Where men and women are now bowing down in worship to the true and living God, our brothers, in darkness, on this very spot once

C. C. BOONE, M. D.

poured out their supplications to gods that could not hear nor see. This came to us as a wonderful inspiration, and should fill us with hope and encouragement and serve as a stimulus for greater efforts on our part in carrying forth the banner of the cross of Jesus Christ to our heathen brethren in the regions beyond us. It is a matter of deep gratitude on the part of the State that the Churches have taken such a deep interest and such an active part in the enlightening and Christianizing of the sons and daughters of our brethren of the interior.

''In all parts of the republic there can be found men and women who have had their training along educational lines in the various schools, colleges and seminaries that operate in connection with and are controlled by the missionary societies, foreign and domestic, of the various Churches represented in this Country.

''We can point with pride to men who today occupy positions of responsibility, trust and dignity in both Church and State, as well as in other walks of life, who have been made what they are through the medium of these schools of the Churches.

''In the President's Cabinet, the portfolios of the general Post-office and Educational Department are held by men of this type. In both branches of the Legislature we find them occupying the front ranks; and so, right on through the various departments of the State we find them.

''In view, then, of the great work that is being done in and for our country by the Churches, it gives me a great deal of pleasure, as representative head of the City of Monrovia, to welcome to this city, the heart, the homes of the people, this great Centennial Celebration of the founding of the Baptist denomination in Liberia. One hundred years of loyal service for the Master. One hundred years of efforts spent in redeeming from heathenism our brothers of flesh and blood. One hundred years of lifting high the standard of the Fatherhood of God and the brotherhood of man. This is a noble record surely! A record of which not only are the Baptists of Liberia proud, but all Liberians rejoice with you in this noble attainment of the mark which, in the providence of God, you have reached."

Centenary Sermon

The "Centenary Sermon" was delivered by the writer of this volume. His text was taken from 1 Sam. 12:7: "Now, therefore, stand still, that I may reason with you before the Lord of all the righteous acts of the Lord which He did to you and your fathers."

Due to repetition of matter found elsewher in this volume, only the first part of this sermon is quoted:

"In the course of human events there comes to us the psychological moment in which we are impelled by some innate motive to stop and carefully analyze the basic principles upon which our success depends. The children of Israel were commanded to 'Stand still and see the salvation of God.' The Lord also said to the erring: 'Come, now let us reason together.' Samuel the prophet of God said to the rebellious house of Israel: 'Now, therefore, stand still, that I may reason with you.' Our Master said, 'For which of you intending to build a tower, sitteth not down first and counteth the cost, whether he have sufficient to finish it.' It is profitable for individuals and nations to take a retrospective view of life. If the ascent towards the goal has been laborious and difficult, pregnant with obstacles, well-nigh inirradicable, one may look backward and gain inspiration by the victories won, or if dejected and overcome by some insatiable desire which has caused your defeat, there is a chance to greatly enhance the prospects of the future by correcting the visible deficiencies. It was for this purpose that the words of our text were uttered by the prophet. Through the seer, God calls the attention of rebellious, ungrateful Israel to all the righteous acts which He had done for them and their fathers. Therefore, brethren, it is for that purpose we have gathered today upon this auspicious occasion, namely: the celebration of the one hundredth anniversary of Providence Baptist Church, that we may mark and emphasize the landmarks set up by them, note their failures, and exult over their ideals and triumphs. Let us here and now, brethren, set up our Ebenezer and thank our benign Creator for the hope, zeal, courage, faith, which He vouched safe unto our illustrious progenitors upon this spot —a spot made sacred by their hallowed tears and blood. The Almighty God has always been nigh unto all who called upon His glorious name in spirit and in truth. He has never failed to give succor if they called upon Him in faith. Yet, many of His subjects are not willing to reciprocate His gracious benefactions. We are not all filled with thankfulness as was Milton when, gazing at God's handiwork, he said:

These are Thy glorious works, Parent of good,
Almighty, Thine this universal frame,
Thus wondrous fair; Thyself how wondrous, then
Unspeakable, who sitt'st above the heavens,
To us invisible or dimly seen, in these Thy lowest works,
Yet these declare
The goodness beyond thought and power divine.

Speak, ye who best can tell, ye sons of light,
Angels; for ye behold Him and, with songs
And choral symphonies, day without night,
Circle His throne rejoicing; ye in heaven,
On earth, join all the creatures to extol
Him first, Him last, Him midst and without end.

"God is talking to us today. He says, through the prophet, 'Now, therefore, stand still, that I may reason with you, and although we can hear no prophet's solemn voice in this age, yet God has always had some manner of communication with His people. One has said 'God, who fragmentarily and multiferiously communicated to us through the prophets, has in these last days revealed Himself through His Son.' We are now reviewing all the righteous acts which He did for our fathers. The greatest act God ever did for our people and the world was to unbosom His only Son to die for the sins of fallen man. The cross stands today as a monument of God's greatest victory—a victory over death, hell and the grave. The story that the cross tells, reaches in the dust of time and pierces into the bounds of infinity. The vastness of the field occupied by the matchless story of the blessed Christ tires the wings of thought, and the grandeur of the theme renews its youth.

"Only a few days after His ignominious death upon the shameful tree and His triumphant ascension into the blissful paradise, according to His promise, the Holy Ghost was poured out upon His consecrated followers. This miraculous fulfillment of God's word produced inexpressible felicity in the hearts of the recipients and caused the conversion of three thousand souls that were added to the Church that same day. Among that vast number of converts were men from almost every nation under heaven. These converts returned to their own countries as forerunners of the Apostles.

"The Apostle Paul was raised up in a miraculous manner, through the providence of God. With his companions, he labored zealously and incessantly until he had preached the Gospel in a short time throughout Asia Minor, Greece and the islands of the Archipeligo. Churches were also established in all the principal cities of those provinces. There is some reason to believe that Paul extended his missionary journeys into Spain and even to England. Matthew, Peter, Jude and Thomas preached effectively in the East, through Mesopotamia, Armenia, Parthia, Persia, and perhaps as far as India, or even China.

"The spread of the Christian religion in the first century is truly wonderful. The triumphs of Julius Caesar, uniting the Roman Empire into one great kingdom, the translation of the Hebrew Bible by Tolemy Philadelphus, and the conquests of Alexander the Great which disseminated the Greek language and made it a vehicle for the spread of the Gospel—these were the leaven in God's hands to disseminate His divine message. The cause must have been divine that enabled men, destitute of human aid, friendless, neither eloquent nor learned, fishermen, publicans and, moreover, Jews; that is, persons despised of all other nations, in so short a time to have persuaded so great a part of mankind to forsake the religions of their fathers and embrace a new religion which is opposed to the natural dispositions of men. But in the hands of these weak, yet heaven-commissioned and heaven-directed instruments, the Gospel is the power of God and the wisdom of God unto salvation. It was the Gospel alone that was destined to bring perpetual peace and good will to all men. The matchless conquests of Xerxes, Hannibal, Napoleon Bonepart, or even Wellington, could not accomplish that end. The poets had sung about peace, but could not produce it. The aristocracy of the Babylonians, the culture of the Greeks, the stern endurance and asceticism of the Romans could not establish that peace for which the world longed. It remained only for the Christ to say, '*Eirenen 'afiemi 'umin, 'eirenen ten 'emen didomi 'umin. Ou' kathos ho kosmos didosin 'ego, didomi 'umin. Me Terasestho humin he kadia mede deiliato*'— 'Peace I leave with you, my peace I give unto you; not as the world giveth, give I unto you. Let not your heart be troubled, neither let it be afraid.'

"Only those who stop to reason and think what God has done for them can come actually in touch with His Son Jesus Christ and obtain the inheritance of the saints. The poet has well said:

> Ye whose hearts are fresh and simple,
> Who have faith in God and nature,
> Who believe that in all ages
> Every human heart is human;
> That in every savage bosom
> There are longings, yearnings, strivings
> For the good they comprehend not;
> That the feeble hands and helpless,
> Groping blindly in the darkness,
> Touch God's right hand in that darkness
> And are lifted up and strengthened.

"I thank God that in the distribution of His many blessings to our fathers, the great land of Africa was not entirely forgotten. Very simple, but touching and powerful, is the record of the first convert of Africa to Christianity. A man of Ethiopia, probably of Meroe, the keeper of the Queen's treasures, was returning from Jerusalem to his own country. He was reading with much pathos—

> Like a sheep being led to the slaughter,
> As a ewe before shearers is dumb,
> He openeth not His mouth.

"The Spirit had already summoned Philip to go down that way, and as he drew near he heard the Eunuch reading these words. Being urged by the Spirit to join himself to the chariot, he then inquired of the honored traveler, 'Understandeth what thou readest'? He made known to Philip that he could not understand without a teacher. He politely, after the African hospitality, invited the stranger to come up and sit with him in his chariot. Philip took the opportunity to discourse with him about the Christ from the very verse which he read. The Eunuch manifested great interest in the new doctrine, and soon believed; then Philip went down with him into the water and immersed him, and the Eunuch went on his way rejoicing.

"Now, we see that the first convert of Africa to the Christian religion was a Baptist. He went forth with joy to spread the good news of the kingdom in the land of Ham. The word of God ran and was glorified. Africa received the Gospel, and, though Athinasius, Bishop of Alexandria, and others, the Church of Jesus Christ developed to mighty proportions. About 320, a Tyrian savant named Meropius sailed down the Red Sea on a tour of exploration. He took with him two youthful nephews—Eudesius and Frumenthius. On the return voyage, the ship touched at an Ethiopian port for water. The savages massacred the crew and passengers. But two escaped. The boys, faithful to the task for which they had been brought, were learning their lessons. The savages, touched by the sight, spared them, but carried them as captives to the King. At Axium, the capitol, their royal master saw their sagacity. He made Eudesius his cupbearer, and Erumenthius the secretary of the treasury. So it was through these two youths that Abyssinia received her first impressions of the Christian religion. The Ethiopians had at last stretched forth their hands unto God. But, notwithstanding the effulgent rays of the Gospel that had been poured forth in Africa, it was destined to soon turn from its first love. Alexandria, becoming the highway for Roman, Egyptian and Tyrian commerce, it soon became voluptuous, unstable, diffident. Explorers from almost every land returned to their homes with their vessels laden with sweet spices, ivory and furs, yet they spoke of Africa as the 'Dark Continent.' Not many years passed before the poor African degenerated into a benighted savage, brought so largely by the baneful influences of the covetous explorer, and partly from lack of pride and the curse of sensuality. Soon the Church is forgotten and Africa, by the highly civilized traders and explorers, is called the 'Dark Continent.' The Continent became so dark that it is famous as a field for plunder and booty. The highly civilized gentlemen of all nations hasten to Africa for gold, rubies, diamonds and, last of all, for slaves.''

Other Addresses

From the address by Miss Martha Robinson:

"Not long ago a lady from the United States said to me, 'I am anxious to see the light shining throught "Dark Africa" '; then other subjects we discussed. A little boy standing nearby said to me after she had left, 'Why do these American people call Africa "dark"? Don't we have the sun, moon and stars to shine for us? Is their sun, moon and stars different from ours?' I said, 'No, they mean Gospel light and education among the heathen.' He said, 'She must say that we need teachers and preachers—Africa is not dark.' So we can see that the boys and girls of Liberia are wide awake and appreciate their Country. As I was about to say, in bygone days, when our fathers were fighting to lay broad and deep the foundations of this little Republic, they had not the privileges that you enjoy today; so, as you have such opportunities, take them without missing one.

"I am forced to say that the young people of Liberia shall keep the Lone Star afloat and wave forever the banner of our Baptist Church. Said one, 'Rejoice, O young man, in thy youth, and let thy heart cheer thee in the days of thy youth; and walk in the ways of thine heart and in the sight of thine eyes, but know thou for all these things God will bring you into judgment. Into judgment—not necessarily into condemnation. God will call us to account for the use we made of these things.' ''

From the address by Mrs. Rachel A. Boone:

"I am happy to know that God saw fit to land me here in Africa at this period of my life. My earnest prayer to God has always been that I might measure up to the standard which He has fixed for me.

"For many reasons, I am proud to be here. First, it is my desire to be here; second, here I can get a better idea of what the world needs to do to fulfill God's command; third, I believe you want me here—some of you at least; fourth, it is my earnest conviction that God wants me here.

"One hundred years ago, as you have already heard from the Centenary Sermon on Sunday morning, there was sent from the First Baptist Church, Richmond, Va., one whose name I heard often memorialized; one whose great work I can never forget; one whose hundredth year of sailing was celebrated at the First Baptist Church, Richmond, Va., by the Board of the Lott Carey Baptist Foreign Mission Convention; one in whose footsteps we tread with trembling and fear, less we fail to accomplish the work God wants us to do. One hundred years ago there came to this spot the beloved, the honored and sainted Lott Carey. Now, from the same city—yea, from the same Church—comes your humble servant, weak, incapacitated, unable to do much, yet, from all indications, it must be that God sent me.

"In Old Testament times, woman was used of God in a miraculous way, and, through her, lasting victories were won. What are some of the glorious epithets by which she is known in the sacred story? Miriam, the ambitious woman (Num. 12:1-2); Deborah, who led the Israelites to victory, is known as the patriotic woman (Jud. 4:4); Abigail, the capable woman (1 Sam. 25:3); Ruth, the faithful woman (Ruth 1:16), and Esther, the self-sacrificing woman. All of these women played a conspicuous part in the evolution of our Christian nation.

"Neither is the New Testament lacking in noble examples of womanhood. The Syro-Phonician woman, the woman of faith; Mary Magdalene, whom Christ Himself gave the highest praise for her honor for Him. And who can ever forget the loving mother of our Blessed Saviour? After Christ had installed His new kingdom into the hearts of men, women were among those who touched the hem of His garments and became the very bedrock in that new Church. She bore our Lord in that lowly manger, then fled with him into Egypt, shed the last tear at the cruel cross, was first at the empty tomb, and was the first messenger of the risen Christ. When Peter was in prison, it was the prayer of the women that turned him out. Would that we had noble women today to emulate the examples of Dorcas, Priscilla, Phebe, who labored hand in hand with the Apostles to scatter the seeds of the Gospel!

"In modern times, missionary women have labored incessantly, at home and abroad, to flood the world with the Gospel light of love and salvation. In a missionary meeting at Clifton Springs, N. Y., a woman rose and told how she had been fifty years a Missionary in Burma; another had been for forty years in French Congo. Have you ever heard how Hessleteen Judson opened Burma at the point of her needle? It was like this: Her husband was thrown into jail for preaching the Gospel, and he had just completed the translation of the Bible into Burmese. Now, how should all of those years of labor be saved? His wife thought upon a plan. So she sewed up the Bible in a pillow and put it under his head, thereby saving the Blessed Word of God to the Burmese people. As teachers in the schools, as nurses in the hospitals, as promulgators of the Word of God, woman has her much-deserved place in modern evangelism.

"The noble women of the past have done well in Church

and State; now, may God help us in our day and generation
to act well our part, for there all the honor lies. What shall
we do for Liberia? What shall we do for the Church? The
harvest field is white, but earnest, consecrated laborers are
very few. We have nothing but words of praise for these
noble women who helped to beautify this house of worship.
Continue the fight, and, as the poet has said:

> Go, labor on, spend and be spent,
> Thy joy to do the Father's will.
> It is the way the Master went;
> Should not the servants tread it still?

> " 'Go, labor on, 'tis not for naught:
> Thine earthly loss is heavenly gain.
> Men heed nor love thee, praise thee not;
> The Master praises; what are men!

> Go, labor on enough while here.
> If He shall praise thee, if He deign
> Thy willing heart to mark and cheer,
> No toil for Him shall be in vain.

> Toil on, and in thy toil rejoice,
> For toil comes rest, for exile home;
> Soon shalt thou heart the Bridegroom's voice,
> The midnight peal, "Behold, I come!"

From address of Deacon A. B. Stubblefield, Jr., on "The
Liberia Baptist Missionary and Educational Convention":

"The organization of the Liberia Baptist Missionary and
Educational Convention dates from April 4, 1882, in 'Good
Hope' Baptist Church, Marshall Junction, Montserrado
County, under the auspices of the Baptist Associations of
Liberia. This representation organized itself into a convention, known as the 'Liberia Baptist Missionary and Educational Convention,' with the late Rev. Joseph J. Cheeseman, LL.D., first President, who served from the time of his
encumbency until his death in the year 1896. The late

Rev. Wesley F. Gibson, D. D., of Marshall, was Vice-President under President Cheeseman.

''The sole object of the Convention is to effect in a more tangible way our purpose of missionary and educational work throughout our denominational limits in Liberia. Thus far, we have succeeded; that is, as far as conditions and means would allow, along the line of Christianizing and evangelizing our heathen brethren.

''Our initiative step in missionary work was the opening of a mission station at Subluehn, about forty miles interior, among the Golahs, under the superintendency of the late Rev. John S. Washington, D. D., who gave undivided service at this station for a period of about ten years, until an uprising among the Aborigines, which necessitated his leaving there, and another site was secured from the Government by purchase, now known as Ricks Institute, about twenty miles from Monrovia. The entire plot is about eleven hundred acres. The Mission work of the Convention is about forty-one years old and was organized on a small scale, with the late Dr. Washington superintendent, as at Subluehn, with a primary educational department taught by Rev. James O. Hayes, D. D., who was the first teacher at Ricks Institute.

''The minds of the leaders of the work expanded to the extent that it was decided to raise the educational standard to a higher basis, with the Rev. Dr. R. B. Richardson, D. D., LL.D., as its first principal, whose unquestionable ability transformed Ricks Institute into the leading educational plant of that day. Students from every county (except Maryland) and the district matriculated there, Aborigine and Americo-Liberian as well. Among some of those who attended were, afterwards, Col. W. D. Lomax, Commissioner Henry B. Ricks, Prof. H. Benedict Hayes, Rev. Daniel James Cheeseman, Prof. Geo. W. Stubblefield, Senator Henry A. Page, Commissioner Washington Seahfa, Hon. Alexander B. Mars, Counselor at Law Emmanuel W. Williams, Captain Arthur B. Gant, your humble servant, and many others whose names we have not space at present to mention.

"The faculty was composed of men of the type of Dr. Richardson, Dr. J. O. Hayes, Prof. H. B. Hayes, Prof. Julius C. Stevens, Prof. Perry O. Gray and others. They did good and profitable work.

"The names of some of the patrons are June Moore, J. J. Cheeseman, J. S. Washington, Henry Moses Ricks, Thos. C. Lomax. John H. Ricks, R. B. Richardson, A. C. Reeves, A. B. Stubblefield, Sr., Wallace F. Moore, William B. Gant, Henrietta Gant, Ada Hayes, Solomon Hill, Sr., Turner Carter, Adeline Moore, Mollie Miller, Laura Hill and others. Baptist Church. They were educated to a certain limit intellectually; but, ah! their equals are not now among us industrially. By the sweat of their face did they eat bread and were able to feed others to this very day by giving large contributions to support education and mission. They toiled, and now, with some, they rest, while with others has come rest; yea, exiled home.

"Since the founding of the Baptist Church in Monrovia, the following places have established said Church in their respective precincts: First Baptist Church, Millsburg; First Baptist Church, Schiefflin; First Baptist Church, Royesville; First Baptist Church, Robertsville; First Baptist Church, Oldest Congo Town; First Baptist Church, Louisiana; First Baptist Church, Clay-Ashland; First Baptist Church, New Georgia; Shiloh Baptist Church, Royesville; Shiloh Baptist Church, Virginia; St. John's Baptist Church, Cheesemanburg; St. John's Baptist Church, Sasstown; Mt. Galillee Baptist Church, Careysburg; Mt. Zion Baptist Church, Robertsport Grand Cape Mount; Zion Grove Baptist Church, Brewerville; Zion Praise Baptist

Church, Bensonville; Bethlehem Baptist Church, Lloyds-
ville; Washington Chapel, Ricks Institute; Macedonia Baptist Church, Barnersville; Morning Star Baptist Church,
Johnsonville; St. Paul's Baptist Church, Arthington; Sa-
lem Baptist Church, Brewerville; Ebenezer Baptist Church,
Caldwell; Union Baptist Church, Dixville; Effort Baptist
Church, Paynesville; Good Hope Baptist Church, Marshall
—twenty-six in all in Montserrado County, the territory of
Robertsport and the territory of Marshall. Taking in the
other territories, the Baptist Churches run up to thirty-
five.''

An address by Mrs. Rachel Cassell, on behalf of Noble
Veterans:

''My first duty, I feel, is to thank you of Providence Baptist Church for assigning our company (the Noble Veterans) a special part on your program during so interesting
a period in the history of your Church. I wish also to con-
gratulate you in the name of our company for being blessed
to witness this the one hundredth anniversary of your
Church. In those years, under God, you have done well.
We join with you in expressions of praises and thanksgiving to God, our common Father and Creator, for all the
blessings and mercies vouchsafed to you, and particularly
for having given you, during the early days of the struggles of this country, such a noble band of women and men
as were Lott and Nancy Carey, Elijah and Rachel Johnson,
Stephen Kiah, the grandfather of late Stephen Allen Benson, second President of Liberia; Colston Waring, the second pastor of this Church; Hilary Teage and his sister,
Colinette, and we cannot forget to mention Susanna Lewis,
who had the very rare privilege and honor of presenting
the Lone Star and Stripes for the first time to Governor
Joseph Jenkins Roberts on the noteworthy occasion of the
public declaration of independence in Monrovia, August

Mrs. Boone's School, Monrovia, Liberia—91 Enrolled, 67 Pure Natives

24, 1847, now known as 'Flag Day.' The great line of
women and men include Jane Rose Roberts, widow of late
President Roberts; Miss Eliza Passaway, one of the pioneers, afterwards becoming Mrs. W. W. Steward, whose
granddaughter and great-grandchildren are still among us.
Then come the Richardsons, Yates, Cheesemans, Stubble-
fields, Browns, all distinguished Baptist Families, some of
whose descendants are still among us, many of whom are
members of this Church today, and are doing good service.''

Mrs. Boone's School at Monrovia

Mrs. Rachel Boone, who had been a special teacher in
Richmond, Va., and had surrendered a salary of $120.00
per month for the promise of $35.00, took hold of the work
with an earnest heart and an active, Christian mind. At
once the school was filled to overflow. Any place you begin
a school in Africa, you will have more students than you
can teach. You do not have to go to the interior to reach
the natives; they come to you.

Very soon the school was above her control, and an assistant teacher, Miss Martha Robinson, a member of the
Providence Baptist Church, was employed. The Baptists
and the people of Monrovia were proud of the school.

Miss Robinson soon decided to quit teaching and take another course in training—''the cottage course.'' Then we
employed Mrs. Taylor. These were two very good teachers
and were thoroughly devoted to their task. We had them
to pay. The Board provided nothing for them.

Headquarters

Besides the school, we were assigned to keep headquarters
for our traveling Missionaries. The hotels and lodging-
houses in Liberia are few, and if they were numerous would
not be very desirable for Missionaries, especially ladies.
We rented a large house at a cost of $500.00 per year, and

fitted up three rooms for visitors at our own expense. We just disliked to see our faithful Missionaries wandering about the streets of Monrovia in the heat or in the rain, with no place to sit down or get a glass of water. Then, if the boat should happen to leave them, they had no place to stay overnight. Besides, they needed some one at Monrovia to pass the cargo through the customs and to attend to the official business of the Mission. Many questions arise that demand immediate action. We did our best in that capacity. My wife was faithful to her task and remained two years overtime.

The American Commission

Many conflicting statements had been sent to America concerning the status of the work in Liberia, so that it became necessary to investigate conditions upon the field in order to properly carry forward the work in Liberia. Accordingly, Dr. C. S. Brown, President of the Lott Carey Baptist Foreign Mission Society, and Dr. A. A. Graham, Corresponding Secretary, were sent out to overlook conditions.

They sent me a cablegram from Liverpool, and I provided a place at Faulkner's Hotel for their accommodation. Their arrival marked a great day in the history of our work in Liberia. We were greatly encouraged by their presence. The building made of cement blocks at Brewerville was dedicated by them. A Board of Control for the government of the field work was organized and your humble servant was appointed chairman, and assigned to Monrovia as headquarters. At this time, the Lott Carey Mission held an enviable position in the Republic. The rather abusive report of Dr. Graham concerning the conditions of the Republic, about which he had absolutely nothing to do, greatly incensed the Liberian people. This caused much retrogression in the work of the Lott Carey Mission at home and upon the foreign field.

Other Missions and Missionaries

I regret very much that space will not permit me to mention all the earnest Missionaries in detail, but I cannot pass from this chapter without making a few personal references. Rev. E. D. Hubbard, at Careysburg, deserves first place. He is teaching the natives how to farm in their own country. He has harnessed the wild horse and put him to work at the plow. With the use of the tractor he is revolutionizing the agricultural work in the Republic. By his own struggles he has cleared a large farm and erected a comfortable dwelling. The school work and Church are also conducted in a splendid way. With proper support, his station might be a modern Tuskegee in Liberia.

Epiphany School, Briely Memorial at Cape Palmas, St. John at Cape Mount, and Brumley on St. Paul River, of the Episcopal Church, are worthy institutions and are doing much to enhance the coming of the Master's kingdom in Liberia.

The Presbyterians are also doing well as a Church in Liberia. The College of West Africa, at Monrovia, under the Methodist Episcopal Church, is performing an invaluable service for the race.

Bishop Brooks erected a monumental building at Monrovia for the African Methodist Church, known as Monrovia College.

The Liberians have a fine school, known as Liberia College. That is the ranking school of the Republic. It was founded by Mr. John Greenleaf, of Boston. The school has rather a checkered history, but its graduates have stood the test and have been some of the most famous leaders of the Republic.

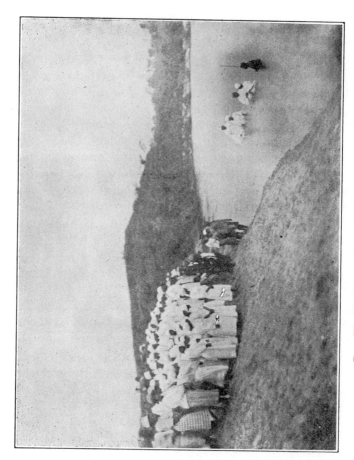

Rev. W. H. Horton Baptizing the Bassa People

When it comes to independent schools, Rix Institute has the first place in the history of Liberian Baptists.

School Statistics, 1925-6

By Whom	Schools	Teachers	Students
Government	56	60	2,000
Baptist	14	36	1,391
Lutheran	8	30	710
Methodist Episcopal Mission	16	63	3,371
Protestant Episcopal	26	34	827
African Methodist	7	14	325
Pentecostal	12	24	225
Independent:			
Dr. H. H. Jones and others	3	8	75

Three Noble Women

Before closing this chapter, I wish to introduce to you three excellent women who exemplified Christ in their lives in Liberia and embellished His kingdom with their consecrated toil.

The first of these is Miss Mary Sharp, of the C. M. E. denomination, who came out to Liberia and remained thirty years. She never returned to the States. She gave all within her for the salvation of the Bassa and Cru people. Dr. W. B. Payne, Secretary of Education, is one of her boys.

Miss E. B. Delaney. She was of excellent Christian character. Her determination was to erect a school in Liberia for the uplift of womanhood. This school now stands at Sueh, under the National Convention, as a lasting monument to her efforts.

Miss Mary Davis. She was perhaps the most influential and the one most dearly beloved by all the Liberian people. Her name was a household word in all the Bassa District. She rallied the Liberian women as only a Nannie Bourrus can in America. Through her influence, she caused to be erected one of the finest school buildings in the Republic, known as the Baptist Industrial Institute, of Bassa.

CHAPTER IX

MEDICINE AND DISEASE

Liberia is a land of wonderful magic and hypnotism. When I visited there in 1906, Rev. J. O. Hayes told me of the excellent native doctors, and I advised him of how we exterminated them in other portions of Africa.

The first contact I had with a native doctor was like this. One day when I had just returned from Monrovia, a man who lived across the street from me came over and informed me that he had been there for me three times before. Said he: ''A woman got shot out on the West Road, and they have been for you three times.'' I was the only physician at Brewerville. That was an important case, so I did not even wait to get a lunch, but rushed out there on my bicycle to see her.

When I arrived, the mother met me and thanked me for coming. She said, however, that having sent three times for me and failing to find me home, she had employed a Congo doctor. What was I to do but turn 'round and come back home? Upon my preparing to depart, she added if the girl did not do well under the other doctor she would send again to call me. The girl recovered.

The next case was a wonderful cure, and I must tell you of it. A woman who was in the ninth month of pregnancy, by some accident had a hemorrhage from the womb. The flow had been continuous for some time, the boys said, who came sixty miles in a canoe for me. It would take me twelve long hours to reach her, even if she was living. As I saw it, the case was beyond medical aid. I could not go. I tried to persuade another physician to go, and he could not. As a last resort, I sent her some adrehlen chloride, with directions for use. I heard nothing from the patient and did not know what had become of her. Shortly after that, I attended a meeting and her husband was there. I hesitated for some time to ask him anything about it, fearing that his wife had died. After a while, however, I ventured to inquire.

And this is what he told me: "After the boys had gone for you, an old native woman passed that way, went in and spoke to my wife. She said, 'What trouble, Mammy?' My wife pointed to the place the trouble was; then told her what was wrong. The old woman said, 'I go help you, Mammy.' She went out to the kitchen and asked for a handful of rice. She put this on to boil. Then she went to the yard and pulled several weeds. These she put with the rice. When they had cooked and were done, she took them to my wife and said, 'Try drink, Mammy.' Mammy could not drink; she had gone too far. Then the old woman begged her to suck and swallow the juice. This she did, and within an hour my wife was feeling better, the flow stopped, and she recovered."

Caesarean Operation

A man by the name of Hawkins came and told me a story that I could not believe without seeing. He informed me that a woman had come to "full time," and the witch doctor had tied the feotus in the womb. He had also warned every one not to touch her upon penalty of death. Therefore, instead of ten lunar months, she had gone eleven. More than that, the foetus had ruptured the abdomen and the feet had protruded five days before, and yet the woman was not delivered and neither was she dead. I went and found his statement correct.

When I first examined the case, I had a mind to keep my hands from it, because there were no assistants and the patient was in daying condition. As I was turning away, the patient drawled out, "Doctor, can't you do something for me?'' I had to yield to her entreaties, for I had spent many sleepless nights in order to be prepared to treat such cases.

I nailed two benches together for my operating table. Then I administered the anesthetic. When she was under the influence sufficiently, I left that part to her father and proceeded to deliver the foetus. I enlarged the rupture that had been made and tried to pull out the foetus with tenaculum forceps, but without result. The mass was gangrenous. I took my hands and soon delivered her of her trouble. It seemed impossible for the patient to live, but by proper sterilization and care, she recovered. For nine days I was both nurse and doctor.

The people in Liberia suffer from yaws, tonsilitis, meningitis, pneumonia, dysentery, smallpox, hookworm, pinworm, all kinds of intestinal worms, the tapeworm especially, guinea worm, malaria, heart leisions, black-water fever. Of course, there are many social diseases brought into the country by foreigners.

Intermittent malaria, I found to be the most treacherous of all the diseases in the country. The patient would insist that he was cured, stop the treatment, and the next day or two afterwards the fever would return with added severity.

Blackwater, or heameturic, fever, the people in Liberia call ''jaundice,'' and treat it by taking calomel. Miss Williamson, of the National Baptist Convention, had a bad case of it, but the Lord helped her. I was her physician.

A solution of sodium bichlorid is said to be a perfect cure for the malady.

I was in Africa twenty-five years, and was never in bed a day from sickness. Perhaps some may accept these few suggestions:

Do not sit outside in the afternoon and let the mosquitoes bite you. Watch the ones with white feet—the ''Anopholes.'' Keep your doors and windows screened. Keep

mosquito net over your bed. Boil all the water you drink.
Take two and one-half grains of quinine every day, whether
you have fever or no. Do not drink lemonade; do not eat
fruit when you first enter the country. Eat American
foods. Never mind the African foods; you will have plenty
of time to try them if you keep your health. Keep your
feet and body dry.

Drugs

You can find growing wild nearly every drug in the
American pharmacopia.

Liberia is waking up to the needs of sanitation and better
facilities for combatting disease. The Government has now
a well-equipped Hospital under Dr. Dingwall, at Monrovia.

The Lutherans have a splendid Hospital at Muhlenburg,
and the National Baptist Convention has built a small Hospital at Monrovia, and Dr. Dinkins has been sent over to
take charge of it. She has since returned, sick.

CHAPTER X

PRESIDENTS OF LIBERIA AND SOME NOTABLE EVENTS DURING
THEIR ENCUMBENCY

1. President J. J. Roberts, from Norfolk, Va. Influenced
to come to Africa through sermon of Lott Carey (1848-56).
Visited America and Europe. France and England acknowledged independence of Liberia.

2. President Stephen Allen Benson (1856-62). Presidents served two years at this time. Navigated St. Paul;
established Hospital; visited Europe.

3. President Daniel B. Warner (1864-68). Time of Civil
War in States.

4. President James S. Payne (1868-72). Preacher, but
took no back seat. English cruiser could not get him to
yield; offered to bombard, and he replied, "Bombard and
be damned!"

5. President E. James Roy (1872). He secured the first
Liberian loan. He and Liberian Consul in London said to
have embezzled it and traded very much of it out. Con-
spired to seize the Bank at Monrovia. Issued proclamation
to extend his term for two years. Deposed, house sacked,
he hides and slipped out at night, ran into ocean, drowned.
He was from Jamaica.

6. President J. J. Roberts called back to office (1872-
1878). He was the "Washington" of Liberia. Again visits
England; sent home on man-o'-war. Government given
lark.

7. President A. W. Gardiner (1878-82). Died in office;
Vice-President Russell finished term. President Gardiner
served third term. National Anthem sung first time under
him.

8. President Alfred Russell (1883).

9. President Hilary Right Johnson (1884-8).

10. President Joseph J. Cheeseman (1888-96). Pure Bassa man. Conducted Grebo War. Died in office.

11. President David Coleman (1896). Fills unexpired term of Cheeseman. Elected 1898. Tried to open interior road; criticised; resigned. Vice-President Gibson takes seat.

12. President Gibson serves unexpired term of Coleman.

13. President Gibson (1904-6). Sent expedition to interior. President Liberia College.

14. President Author Barclay (1904-8). Term of President now four years. Emigrated to Liberia from Jamaica when a small boy seven years old. Visited England. Secured Sir Harry Johnson loan. Rubber farm and goldmine concessions. President Liberia College.

15. President Daniel Edward Howard (1912-20). The war President. Conducted Cru War; called the "Chester" from U. S. A. to help. Nobly assisted by Col. Chas. Young, who reorganized and trained frontier force. Conducted Golah War. Disarmed the natives. Country in perfect peace first time in history. Appointed Boundary Commission. Settled boundary disputes. Sent Boundary Commissioners to take detonated stations. Joined the Allies in the great European war. Sixty Germans deported under escort of frontier force and Liberian soldiers. German submarine visits Liberia. This was the greatest day I ever saw in this world. It had every appearance of Judgment Day. I was then Secretary of the American Legation.

Submarine Appears

Early one morning, without a particle of warning, there was news of a German submarine down near the Lighthouse, visible. I need not tell you everybody that could walk went down there to see it. There she was, indeed and in truth. Germany had published that she would send it.

We waited as long as we could, and then we turned towards the White House to see what was going on. I met good Bishop Camphor, who, like all the rest of us, was terribly upset. He begged me to go up into the Mansion to see if we could hear any news. President Howard and his wife had always been stanch friends of mine. He greeted us cordially. Of course, I was then in the diplomatic circles. President was calm and determined. Mr. T. J. R. Faulkner, who was intercessor, was busy taking messages from the President to the submarine, and vice versa. The submarine had already sunk Liberia's only gunboat and held the captain prisoner. One man jumped off and swam ashore. He brought word of its arrival.

The captain demanded that Liberia demolish the French wireless. President Howard and his Cabinet refused to do so. They then sent back word that if Liberia failed to dismantle the wireless by 4 o'clock P. M. that they would themselves destroy it. Word was sent to go ahead, that Liberia would have nothing to do with the French wireless towards destroying or dismantling it.

We suspended operations at the Legation to watch the outcome, save for a few cablegrams framed for U. S. A. As I sat at my home on Crown Hill after dinner, just before the time for the submarine to begin her bombardment, hundreds of people were running down behind the hills, some going on boats up river, some with chairs in one hand and clothes, etc., in the other. Some with the sick upon their backs; others, too sick to walk, had a chair in which they would sit a minute, then get up and hop a few yards and sit down again. I quieted a lot of them by sitting and reading my paper. They exclaimed when they saw me, "That man is reading the paper—ah, ha!" I explained to them that the submarine would not bombard the city, but simply tear down the French wireless. This was solace to hundreds

House Struck by German Submarine, in which Three Persons were Killed

of weary hearts at that time. I was in the Legation, and they knew that what I said was official.

About 3:30 I moved down the road toward the French wireless; so much Daniel Boon-like, I wanted to see the thing done. I was the closest man to the submarine except Mr. Faulkner, who was on board the submarine.

At 4 P. M. to the minute they began firing. The French had taken their engine down and moved it away and taken away all of their explosives. They remained at their posts at the wireless. The firing was great. You could see the flash, and the roar sounded like two or three claps of thunder all in one.

They did not injure the wireless very much before they discovered the Burutu, an English steamer, coming from the South. They rushed out to destroy it and promised to be back and finish their job. The Burutu came steadily along. I ran down upon the beach to see the battle—surely Liberia was in war! But the English merchantmen had trained gunners upon them in those days; and all at once her big gun sang out and the shell struck near the submarine. We noticed that the submarine would not approach the cargo boat. Then, as the Burutu steamed away in the sunset. she and the submarine kept up firing until way into the night we could hear the reports down the coast. We learned by wireless in a few days that the Burutu struck the periscope of the submarine and it could not submerge. The submarine was gone, and I rushed up home to prepare for the night, and behold! several bullets from the submarine had crashed into my neighbor's house and killed two of his children, mortally wounded his poor mother, and broken the arm of his sister-in-law. I had to be undertaker and prepare the little ones for burial. They were terribly mutilated. (See photo of the house that was struck by a shell from the submarine.)

Death and Starvation.

Can you imagine what we did in Liberia when we had been dependent for food upon the German and English ships? May God help you, reader; and though you may be cast in prison or upon some lonely island, may you never be in the condition we poor Missionaries were at this time.

For months not a dust of flour, not a soda cracker, or even a tin of sardines could be found. At the market, if a bit of meat was brought there for sale, you could see great men contending with each other for it. They would catch hold of the same shoulder of meat and would not release their grip until the meat was weighed in some way and each had his part. No one at home gives us credit for standing at our post in those perilous times. There is only one who thinks of it, and, when the account is reckoned, always gives us the credit for being faithful.

When that wretched war was over, Hon. C. D. King, President-elect, and Senator Dunbar were sent as envoys to the League of Nations. Liberia was refunded for the damages incurred by the submarnie bombardment. With all of this, you know that President D. E. Howard was glad to be rid of the war and to retire and take some rest.

President Charles Dunbar Burges King

He was the best-prepared of all the Presidents, having served in many responsible positions in the Government, even Secretary of State. He had been in Government employ for seventeen years previously. He was a graduate of Liberia College. He was born in Freetown, Sierra Leone, and was early brought to Monrovia. He is a conscientious, energetic, scholarly genius.

At the beginning of his office, while President-elect, he was called to visit America and seek to secure a loan of $5,000,000 from the American Government.

The Garvey Movement

In 1923, Liberia was confronted with the Garvey Movement. Marcus Garvey, elected by a few enthusiastic admirers as the Potentate of Africa, had so bewitched the public mind with his Ciceroan oratory that great crowds were
shouting his jubilant praises from Liberty Hall, New York
City. The Black Star Line was organized and a steamer
was put on between the United States and Cuba. This ship
was manned by Colored seamen. Marcus Garvey was a
Jamaican. Another son of thunder, Marshall, from Jamaica, landed in Liberia and carried the Country by storm,
insomuch that the Mayor of Monrovia, Gabriel Johnson,
came over from Liberia as a delegate to the great Convention in New York. He was elected Vice-Potentate. When
he returned to Liberia, an enthusiastic welcome was given
him in the Representative Hall. Soon after this, ''Marshall,'' the evangelist of Negro domination in Liberia, was
convicted of murder and hanged.

Coming of the Commission

While President King was away and Secretary Edwin
Barclay was acting President, a Commission was sent by
Marcus Garvey to Liberia to arrange terms of co-operation
between Liberia and the Kingdom of Marcus Garvey. I
was in New York, and welcomed Mr. Johnson to New York
by escorting him and introducing him to the Baptist State
Sunday School Convention of New York. I was also in
Monrovia, Liberia, when the Commission arrived.

An overcrowded meeting was given them in the spacious
Methodist Episcopal Church, Monrovia. Everybody was
there. The Commissioners acquitted themselves as states-
men. There was one woman. The most distinguished
speaker of the group was Mr. Polston, from North Carolina.
He used wise and persuasive arguments. He acknowledged

that the movement had made mistakes, because, he said,
"When Mr. Garvey first entered America no one would
listen to him but the man upon the street, the unprepared;
but now that he is being heard by the leading men of America, the prospects are brighter and the early mistakes are
being corrected, and unprepared men are being replaced
by well-qualified men as fast as they can be secured." His
speech won the Liberian people.

Things went well. The women were organized into an
auxiliary and Ex-President Howard's wife was elected
President. The fever ran so high at Brewerville, Clay-
Ashland, Arthington and Monrovia, that one was under a
kind of smothering ostracism who did not rave with delight
over the movement. All of us encouraged it and hoped for
the best.

Opposition from Without

Shortly after the Commission departed, Liberia had
many visits from British and French men-o'-war. Soon it
was whispered around that stubborn opposition had been
presented by England and France to the acceptance of the
Garvey Movement. A halt must be made if Liberia was to
sustain its integrity. It had been announced in Liberty
Hall, New York, that "When we enter Africa, we will not
ask the white man to get out, but we will put him out."

Not wishing to destroy the Negro Republic that she had
striven so hard to foster, it is reported that the United
States Government refused for a while to grant passports
to any person going to Liberia except Bishops and Missionaries.

In Liberia, the incoming steamers were guarded by po-
licemen, and any one claiming allegiance to the Garvey
Movement was returned to the United States. Several were
deported from Monrovia.

What did Liberia have to say about the "movement"?

President King, at a public meeting, said, "Take the Marcus Garvey Movement—one need not undertake impossible things. You have heard of companies being organized in Germany (Janzen, West & Co.) and in England (Patterson Zokonis Company), and in America (Standard Oil Co.), and the like; but you never heard of a company including the entire white race. How can any man unite all the Colored people of the world into one company? Gentlemen, it does not seem plausible."

President King, intellectual and progressive, began to forge ahead. Boundary Commissioners were appointed, automobile roads were opened, and the sidewalks in Monrovia were curbed.

Monrovia Lighted

The City of Monrovia that had been in darkness for one hundred years was lighted by electricity. This was done, however, through the help and ingenuity of Hon. Thomas J. Faulkner, who came originally from North Carolina, U. S. A. It is magnificent at night to see from the harbor the City of Monrovia lighted by electricity.

Customs Exports and Destination

To	1922	1925
England	$274,404.27	$393,885.99
Germany	499,822.51	855,219.24
Holland	195,497.02	292,013.93
Spain	....	5.28
France	999.52	606.00
U. S. A.	2,037.32	254,388.98
Other countries	72,052.14	114,933.18

Customs Imports and Origin

From	1922	1925
England	$647,515.76	$728,372.28
Germany	229,915.37	704,881.97
Holland	147,393.56	192,500.40
Spain	55.54	8,310.98
France	22,877.79	....
U. S. A.	131,178.34	210,708.36
Other countries	122,579.16	246,812.13

Principal Exports

The principal exports are coffee, rubber, ivory, palm kernels, palm oil, piasava, colanuts, cocoa beans, calabar beans, ginger.

Principal Imports

The principal imports are lumber, cement, corrugated iron, tools, machinery, automobiles, groceries, cotton goods, spiritous liquors.

Solomon Porter Hood and Firestone Rubber Company

Rev. Solomon Porter Hood, American Minister and Consul-General to Liberia, succeeded Minister J. L. Johnson. Minister Hood had the real interest of Liberia always upon his mind and heart. He often exclaimed at public banquets that "I have no ambition to become known here as a public orator. Others have brought into this country various interests. Bishop Brooks has brought to us a magnificent school building, Monrovia College; Dr. Boone has brought to us the great Lott Carey Mission, and as a physician is seeking to heal the wounds of the suffering; but I hope to be the economic saviour of the Republic."

Night and day he worked away doing his best to convince the Liberian people that it was the gateway to economic success to grant a concession to Mr. Harvey Firestone, of America. Syndicates of other countries had entered Liberia, but no American company of notable caliber had invested in the Republic. After much palaver, both in America and Liberia, the contract was signed and Firestone entered. He has presented me one of his new books, "Men and Rubber." Therefore, I can do no better than to quote from his own words.

"In December, 1923, my attention was called to the Country of Liberia, on the West Coast of Africa. I sent a representative to Liberia, where he found 2,000 acres planted in 1910 with hevea trees, which are the standard and best producing species and used throughout the East. This plantation had been abandoned shortly after the war began, and its lease reverted to the Liberian Government. Although it had received no attention for several years, our representative tapped the trees and found the flow of latex equal to or better than that of the Far East. He returned to America at once and reported that climate, soil and labor conditions in Liberia were equal to, if not better than, those in any part of the Eastern rubber-producing areas where he had spent seventeen years in rubber cultivation.

"In April, 1924, he, accompanied by two experienced rubber planters and two other men who had spent several years on the West Coast of Africa and Liberia, returned to Liberia to make a thorough survey. They explored hundreds of miles into the interior to determine the topography and suitability of the country for rubber-growing, and also to find out about the availability and conditions of labor. It is estimated that there are 2,000,000 natives in Liberia. They found the native population to be of a healthy and vigorous type and apparently willing workers. He took over the 2,000-acre plantation, cleared the undergrowth, and began tapping. In a few months he had confirmed our prelininary reports as to the possibilities of the economical production of rubber. We also did some preliminary work in clearing the jungle, in order to determine the character of the labor and the actual cost of planting. With this expedition, I also sent a representative to Liberia to confer with the Liberian Government as to an agreement to take over lands for rubber-planting on a large scale. The outcome of that agreement I have already referred to.

"Before the Committee on Interstate and Foreign Commerce of the House of Representatives, I said, in part, on January 15, 1926: 'It is my opinion that if America is to attain any degree of independence in its source of rubber, as well as other materials which are now in the hands of foreign monopoly, our government must give proper encouragement to capital and must assure the industries interested that it will lend its utmost assistance in protecting our investments. This particularly applies to rubber, for it is necessary to make a large capital investment.

" 'I recognize the difficulties involved in this suggestion. I do not presume to speak with reference to our foreign policy. Surely, however, it is practicable to recommend that our Government take active steps to remove those laws in the Philippine Islands which are an effective barrier against large-scale development of rubber plantations there, and to enact such laws as would encourage the investment of capital in the Philippine Islands. An awakened public sense of the dangers which threaten our sources of supply may be regarded of the highest importance. I do not favor a subsidy in the form of an import tax or in any other form whatsoever, nor do I favor any measures which may be regarded in any sense retaliatory towards the British Government or any other foreign country.

" 'The proper solution of the problem, in my opinion, is the investment of American capital on a large scale in plantations for rubber production. These investments must largely be made in foreign countries, at great distances and in large amounts. It is an industry of large figures. This is illustrated by the fact that the latest figures available indicate the investment by British investors of the huge sum of $500,000,000 in the rubber-producing industry. The American people will make the necessary investments if their capital in these far-off countries only if they feel assured of the sympathetic support of their own government, and in my opinion our Government should do everything in its power, consistent with its foreign policies, to encourage such investments.'

"What I said before the Congressional Committee applies particularly to Liberia and the Philippines. We have been offered concessions in the Philippines which we may or may not take up, according to the assurance that the terms will be carried out.

"Liberia is a child of the United States; it is the result of a philanthropic movement in this country, begun more than a hundred years ago, to return the Negro slaves to their African homeland. This territory was bought with American money, the government was set up with American money, and on the American model. In an official communication to President Roosevelt, in 1909, Secretary of State Elihu Root stated: 'Liberia is an American Colony. . . . It is unnecessary to argue that duty of the United States toward the unfortunate victims of the slave trade was not completely performed in landing them upon the coast of Africa, and our Nation rests under highest obligation to assist them, so far as they need assistance, towards the maintenance of free, orderly and prosperous civil society. The interest of the people of the United States also furnishes strong reasons for helping to maintain this Colony, whose success in self-government will give hope and courage, and whose failure would bring discouragement to the entire race.'

"This communication was in connection with an investigation into the conditions of Liberia by an official Government Commission, which inquiry had been requested by the Liberians in an application to the United States for aid in maintainng its independence and political integrity, and the loan of its assistance in administering its financial and governmental affairs. This plea was the outgrowth of continual disputes with the Colonial Governments of their neighbors, Great Britain and France, who the American Commission found had been constantly encroaching upon Liberian territory.

"The Commission recommended that the United States officially assist Liberia in maintaining its boundaries, reorganizing its finances, and developing its hinterland. It was cordially supported by the State Department and President Taft, who wrote Congress: 'I trust that the policy of the United States toward Liberia will be so shaped as to fulfill our National duty to the Liberian people, who by the effort of this Government, and through the material support of American citizens, were established upon the African coast and set on the pathway to sovereign Statehood.'

"In commenting upon Liberian people, the American Commission said it was 'impressed with the dignity and intelligence of the representatives of the Government with whom it had dealings. . . . The Liberians are not a revolutionary people. Since the beginning of their national life, they have maintained the forms of orderly Government.' . . . Despite frequent assertions to the contrary, Liberia is not bankrupt. . . . In contrast to the natural wealth of the country, its national debt ($1,300,000 in 1909) is very small.

"The Commission points out that the maintenance of its borders, chiefly as a result of the partition of Africa by European powers, has kept Liberia occupied politically to the detriment of its commercial and industrial development. To the west, Liberia has the British Colony of Sierra Leone, also established as a Colony of freed black men; on the north and east are the French Colonies of Guinea and the Ivory Coast.

"The 43,000 square miles composing Liberia lie well within the world's rubber belt, extending from four to eight degrees north of the equator. It is bounded for 350 miles on the west by the Atlantic Ocean, and is within 4,000 miles of New York by direct steamer route. There is an average of more than one steamer a day calling at Monrovia (named after President Monroe), the Capital and principal port, and it is a regular port for two steamship lines to America and six to Europe and England. It has numerous rivers, navigable for from twenty-five to ninety-five miles from the sea. Its land transportation is, however, totally undeveloped, there being no railroads and only a few miles of passable roadways. Road building, harbor improvement, and installation of lines of communication are in my plan.

"The land, for the most part, is well drained, consisting of gently sloping hills, with intervening, wide, winding depressions. Forests cover almost the entire area, but there is comparatively a small amount of 'big bush' or virgin jungle. This is due for the most part to the rotating system of cultivation practiced by the natives for centuries. Each family clears and plants a new area each year, refusing to use the same cleared land until seven years or more have elapsed. *This system has not robbed the soil of its fertility, and at the same time has made the work of clearing for rubber plantations less expensive, because secondary growth timber is much easier to remove than virgin jungle.

"Health conditions in Liberia are exceptional for the tropics. The natives are strong and healthy. Their villages are clean and as sanitary as is possible under primitive conditions. It is not uncommon for a native carrier or porter to travel thirty miles in ten hours with a burden of forty to sixty pounds balanced upon his head. Among 500 natives employed upon our 2,000-acre plantation, fifteen miles inland, there was only one case of illness last year (1925). This is a remarkable record, for it is not uncommon among the plantation operations of the Far East to have 30 per cent of the labor force absent at one time on

---

*The natives have these rotating crops because they know no way of fertilization for the used lands, except to let it grow up, cut it down, and burn the growth to manure their crops.

account of illness. Sleeping sickness, yellow fever and other plagues are rare in Liberia, although quite prevalent at other places on the West Coast of Africa.

"Under the terms of an agreement entered into with the Government of the Republic of Liberia, I have been granted 1,000,000 acres of land most suitable for the production of crude rubber; another lease for a like period upon the plantation of 2,000 acres, which was planted fifteen years ago and is in full bearing; and an agreement for the general public improvement of the Country, such as the construction of port and harbor facilities, roads, hospitals, sanitation, lines of communication, and the development of hydroelectric power.

"The cost of reclaiming the jungle and bringing rubber into bearing in Liberia will be a minimum of $100 per acre, or a total of $100,000,000 to develop the full acreage of our lease. To operate such a development at capacity will require the employment of 350,000 native laborers. For the last year, our factories have been receiving shipments of highest grade rubber from this plantation. Clearing operations were begun upon thousands of acres of land several months ago. A large labor force has already been organized, and a staff of expert planters and their assistants are already on the grounds.

"The operating plan for the first year calls for an organization consisting of a medical staff, sanitary engineer, mechanical engineer, architect and builder, soil expert, foresters and their staff, as well as twenty planting units, each in charge of an expert planter and his assistants. These men will recruit and organize the thousands of native laborers required.

"I believe that we can build up Liberia through our own operations to a point where, in addition to being our great rubber source, will also be a large market for American goods. This will be serving the people in a practical way."

Through the entrance of Firestone Rubber Company into Liberia, in 1925, the customs receipts advanced $30,000 over the previous year. Some have wondered if Firestone would not monopolize the Liberian Government, but in a conference with Mr. Harvey Firestone at the Jefferson Hotel, in Richmond, Va., he assured me that no such idea had ever been entertained by the company.

When I mentioned the fact that we had been engaged for ten days at Hampton Institute helping Mr. Sibley to make textbooks for Liberia, Mr. Firestone remarked that "That is my educational contribution to Liberia." To follow up the Firestone plantation with the Gospel of Christ and Mission Schools is an open door for evangelization of Liberia.

CHAPTER XI

LIBERIAN GOVERNMENT AND THE ADVANTAGES OFFERED

The framers of the Constitution made it impossible for any white person to own property in Liberia or to become a citizen of the country. All of the officers and lawmakers are Colored people. The Government is democratic in nature and fashioned after the United States.

They have a President, Vice-President, Secretary of State, Attorney General, Secretary of the Treasury, Treasurer, Secretary of Education, Secretary of Interior, Secretary of War and Navy, Secretary of Agriculture, and Financial Adviser.

The Legislature (so called in Liberia) makes the laws, and their Representatives are elected by the citizens. I think there is a property qualification for voters.

The Supreme Court is presided over by Chief Justice F. R. L. Johnson, one of the most scholarly and certainly one of the most affable gentlemen of the Republic.

The Courts of Law are conducted in a systematic way, and White and Colored offenders are brought to justice. Several nations have demurred at the decisions of the Liberian Courts, but when the evidence has been taken before the Foreign Courts, in every instance the Liberian decisions have been sustained.

Foreigners are permitted to lease property in Liberia, and many take advantage of this privilege. As in other parts of the world, they do a thriving business in Liberia. (See the reports of the Customs.) Shall I inform my readers that the white people go to Liberia and lease the land and do the business for the Country? They have the bank —Bank of British West Africa. The Germans had a bank before the European War. They have the Cable station (French).

Hon. T. J. R. Faulkner owned the ice plant, electric lights, and the hotel. Furthermore, he taught all the boys how to run their steam launches and mechanics. He was a Colored man.

The big white merchants have sent the Colored business men to the wall. The well-equipped white doctors (French and German) have taken the medical profession. I did hear of a German farmer entering the country, but he had not made much success in 1926.

Liberia furnishes the best field in all the world for the enterprising Colored man. What can we do and what is to be gained? That question has been asked me an hundred times within the past twelve years.

Are you a barber? There is not a decent shop in the City of Monrovia. Yes, you may shave Colored and white people. Liberia permits no segregation; you must treat all alike.

Are you any kind of a mechanic? The Government is in need of competent mechanics; Firestone pays big money.

Are you a banker? The Republic needs you, instead of having to bear heavy burdens from white bankers.

Do you know how to grow cane and make sugar? Hurry to Liberia! There are millions of acres of rich land waiting for you.

Do you know the dairy business? Please go to Liberia; there is the best grazing land upon the Continent of Africa. And there the flies do not kill the cattle as they do in the Congo.

Can you farm? Do you know how to grow cabbage, lettuce, cucumbers, pineapples, bananas and oranges? Liberia is the place for you. There are eight or ten steamers a week in the harbor of Monrovia to which you may sell such produce at an extra price. The people at the Spanish Islands, Tineriffe and Las Palmas, do nothing but grow such vegetables and fruits for the steamers. What is the matter with Liberia? Her doors are open to the energetic and frugal.

Are you a baker? Now is your time to sell cakes and pies to the many waiting customers of the Republic.

Do you know how to run a laundry? O for the first brave man who will begin a steam laundry in Monrovia!

Are you a shoemaker? Bring some good leather and stop the ravage of hook worm by taking the feet of the honest men from the bare grounds.

Are you a fisherman? Are you afraid of the water? Are you afraid of plenty of money? Can you manage your own business, or do you need a guardian? You must fish in the ocean, not in small creeks; you must know how to do big things and a fortune is yours!

Please do not go to Liberia looking for a job. Carry your job with you and the people of the Republic will receive you with open arms.

Are you a teacher? There are millions of African people in Liberia who have never seen a book. Are you a Missionary? May the Lord help you to gird up your loins for "the day is far spent."

"Say not ye, There are yet four months and then cometh harvest. Behold, I say unto you, Lift up your eyes and look on the fields, for they are white already to harvest."

Ethiopia is now stretching forth her hands unto God. Reader, will you answer the Macedonian call? What will you do to save Liberia?

Already Liberia is ablaze with enthusiasm, and signs of plenty and prosperity everywhere abound.

Through the influence of Firestone, we understand, Liberia has obtained a substantial loan, paid off American and other indebtedness.

President King has toured Europe and has been cordially and diplomatically received according to his station as President of a great Nation. He has been elected and inaugurated for the third time. Hope has sprung from the dust and the dream of the sainted seers of the Republic, Hilary Teage, Elijah Johnson and Lott Carey has been at last realized.

> Dim though the night of these tempestuous years,
> A Sabbath dawn over Africa appears.
> Then shall her neck from Europe's yoke be freed,
> And healing arts to hideous arms succeed.
> At home the bonds of peace her tribes shall bind,
> Commerce abroad espouse them with mankind,
> While pure religion's hand shall build and bless
> The Church of God amidst the wilderness.
>   —*Montgomery.*
>   *Amen.*

INDEX

Page

CHAPTER I
Causes that Led to the Formation of the Liberian Republic

CHAPTER II
Founding the Colony

CHAPTER III
Foura Bay—Grand Bassa—Mesurado

CHAPTER IV
Ashmun and the Colonists

CHAPTER V
Lott Carey, His History, Heroism and Sudden Death

CHAPTER VI

The Country and Its Inhabitants

CHAPTER VII

Setting up a Stable Government

CHAPTER VIII
Missionaries and Schools

CHAPTER IX
Medicine and Disease

CHAPTER X
Presidents of Liberia and Some Notable Events During Incumbency

CHAPTER XI

Liberian Government and the Advantages Offered.

LIST OF ILLUSTRATIONS